ANTIQUITIES OF THE
IRISH COUNTRYSIDE

Antiquities
of the Irish Countryside

SEÁN P. Ó RÍORDÁIN

Fifth edition

revised by

RUAIDHRÍ DE VALERA

Methuen
LONDON AND NEW YORK

First published in 1942 by
Cork University Press
Second edition 1943
Third edition published in 1953 by
Methuen & Co. Ltd
11 New Fetter Lane, London EC4P 4EE
Fourth edition 1965
Fifth edition 1979

Published in the USA by
Methuen & Co.
an associate company of Methuen, Inc.
733 Third Avenue, New York, NY 10017

Typeset by Red Lion Setters
Printed in Great Britain by
Richard Clay (The Chaucer Press) Ltd, Bungay
Plates printed by
Fletcher & Son Ltd, Norwich
ISBN 0 416 85630 6 (hardback edition)
ISBN 0 416 85610 1 (paperback edition)

CONTENTS

LIST OF FIGURES

LIST OF PLATES

The Publishers wish to thank the individuals and organizations given below for permission to reproduce the photographs in their possession.

Between pages 40-41

FROM THE PREFACE
TO THE FIRST EDITION
(*Cork University Press, 1942*)

This booklet is not intended for specialists in archaeology. Its purpose is to give some answer to the questioning man in the street, who asks the archaeologist for a simple explanation of some monument which he has noticed in the countryside and which is, in all probability, a typical example of a class of antiquity widespread throughout Ireland.

The question usually concerns an individual structure, be it fort, souterrain, stone circle, or other antiquity, of which the archaeologist, lacking evidence which excavation might yield, can say little. He can, however, explain at some length what is known of this *type* of monument. So that such information may be available in a convenient printed form it is proposed to give an outline here of the present state of knowledge concerning those classes of antiquities most frequently met with in the Irish countryside, and it is hoped that our brief notes will make them intelligible to the inquiring layman. Monuments, (churches, high crosses, round towers, and so on) belonging specifically to Early Christianity are not dealt with here, since their study involves the subjects of architecture and art rather than archaeology proper, and it is proposed to confine our survey to the types of monuments most common throughout the country.

Since this booklet is for the general reader, who may have no ambitions or opportunity to delve deeply into the voluminous archaeological literature which might be invoked on each of the topics covered, it is not intended to encumber the text pages with references. Should the reader wish more fully to acquaint himself with the subject, the Bibliography at the end may be found useful. With the aid of this, he should be in a position to evaluate for himself the evidence produced by excavation and by field surveys.

It is the hope of the writer that, having read the pages that follow, the reader may be stimulated to seek for himself examples of the antiquities therein described. Should he wish to do so, he is strongly advised to procure for himself a copy of the 6-inch Ordnance Survey Sheet covering the district in which he is interested. The maps are invaluable and must serve as the basis for any proposed Field Survey. While on some sheets the sites of almost all monuments are recorded, on others the omissions will be found to be numerous, this being particularly true of mountainous areas. The enthusiast with a flair for field work can do immense service to archaeology by undertaking an accurate survey of all the ancient remains in some one district. Such a survey calls for detailed plans and descriptions of all sites, whether recorded by the O.S. or not. Its careful compilation will, in many instances, bring to notice monuments unknown to Irish Archaeology, while it should, in any case, serve to make more complete our still very inadequate knowledge of field antiquities particularly in the matter of the distribution of the different types.

PREFACE TO THE FIFTH EDITION

More than a quarter of a century has elapsed since the late Professor Seán P. Ó Ríordáin completed the third edition of his *Antiquities of the Irish Countryside*. Throughout that time it has admirably served its primary purpose of informing 'the questioning man in the street' as its author himself had intended. It also proved to be a valuable synthesis for students of Irish archaeology as the success of the fourth edition as a University Paperback so amply showed. With the passage of time as Ó Ríordáin himself anticipated, new discoveries and advances in archaeology inevitably called for additions and alterations and it is the purpose of the present edition to meet this demand. The task has been made more onerous and at the same time more interesting by the expansion of Irish archaeological work during the last twenty-five years — in the fostering of which Ó Ríordáin himself played such a major rôle.

In preparing this edition I have sought to retain the original author's approach and many passages of the text remain virtually unaltered. The chapter arrangement follows his save that the sections dealing with Fields, Roads and Linear Earthworks are taken out of the chapter on Forts to form a new chapter of their own.

Since the field antiquities reflect, in many cases, episodes in the story of Ireland's past I have added an Introduction which seeks to synthesize these episodes and relate the various monument types to them. In doing so an attempt is made to see the monuments and the episodes with which they are connected in a geographical setting and see the societies who built them as real people, however shadowy and uncertain the picture may often be. Such an approach is, of course, not new but as one works through the various stages of the story it becomes clear that it has been very unevenly attempted as yet in Ireland. For many episodes opportunities for the exploitation of this approach are manifest through such techniques as detailed mapping, soil and vegetation studies etc. The recognition of natural regions and barriers and their effect on settlement can yield useful results. The regions occupied by different groups can tell us a good deal about economic requirements and the capabilities of the various groups to exploit and sometimes alter their environment. The effect of other contemporary groups on the extent of settlement, however difficult to assess, cannot be ignored. In the present state of knowledge conclusions must often be tentative and the sketch given in the Introduction should be read with this constantly in mind. It is given, not with any claim to finality but in the hope of stimulating interest and research in what must surely be in the future a fertile field.

In view of modern trends which eschew the idea of invasion some of what I have written will doubtless be dismissed as outdated 'invasionism'. It is true that often in the past the beginnings of new types in a given area were too readily assumed to represent invasions. It is equally true that the arrival of totally new ranges of monuments and material has been explained as some vague spread of ideas with no appreciable immigration. As always the truth lies between. I can only say that within the narrow limits of the pages of the Introduction I have tried to indicate how far the various episodes suggest a sizeable number of immigrants. That some colonization and lesser immigration took place need cause no surprise, for such are well in evidence in both Britain and Ireland in historic times. It is of course entirely another matter to decide whether any incursion was warlike or peaceful and on this in prehistory we have seldom sufficient evidence to pass judgement. I trust also that in speaking of new arrivals it is clear that the indigenous population would normally have survived and doubtless have influenced in their own way subsequent developments.

Those who are familiar with archaeological literature of recent times may be surprised or disappointed that I have given short shrift to theories concerning exact orientation and standardized measurement in regard to megalithic monuments — tombs, circles and alignments. These theories often imply a deep and detailed knowledge of complex astronomical phenomena and a grasp of mathematical procedures on the part of man in megalithic times. They are supported by an array of figures, formulae, statistics and computer procedures with which most archaeologists are less than adequately acquainted. However, all too often the mathematics can be shown to be faulty and logic and simple commonsense to be lacking. There is now available a large body of evidence from Ireland which indicates a broad adherence to general orientation customs in certain classes of tombs and circles which is readily explained in terms of the general knowledge of ordinary country folk of the main directions such as we would nowadays call North, South, East and West. Many Christian graves and churches are roughly aligned east and west and the ill luck attending the man who extends his house westwards is proverbial still in parts of Ireland. No detailed observation or precise alignment is implied in these and no such implication is required to explain the orientation of megalithic monuments. One wonders if it is not part of a tendency apparent in many spheres in recent times — to seek after and even invent the spectacular, the mysterious, let alone the occult, beloved of modern media of communication. There are surely enough mysteries in life without creating more. Knowledge of our roots should be firmly grounded not set in fantasy. I think Ó Ríordáin, *ar dheis Dé go raibh sé*, would approve.

University College   Ruaidhrí de Valera
Dublin

April 1978

ACKNOWLEDGEMENTS

I must first offer my sincerest gratitude to Mrs Gabriel Ó Ríordáin, who honoured me by entrusting the preparation of this new edition of her late husband's book to me. I wish also to thank the members of the Department of Archaeology, University College, Dublin for much help and valuable discussion on various sections. I am particularly indebted to my constant collaborator in the Megalithic Survey, Mr Seán Ó Nualláin, Archaeological Officer in the Ordnance Survey. His assistance and advice added much not only to the chapters on Megalithic Tombs, Standing Stones, Stone Alignments and Stone Circles which are his special field, but also to the work as a whole. I have drawn freely on his unrivalled knowledge of field antiquities throughout all Ireland and benefited greatly from his ideas and criticism, both generously given.

Since footnotes are not used I offer my apologies and gratitude to all workers in Irish Archaeology on whose published work I have drawn. To all those throughout the length and breadth of Ireland who in many ways made possible the discovery and survey of our monuments I share a common debt with all field archaeologists. Finally, I wish to thank the publishers, Messrs Methuen & Co. for their boundless patience and consideration.

R. de V.

PUBLISHER'S NOTE

We deeply regret the death of Professor de Valera which occurred before the publication of this new edition, and we should like to thank Mr Seán Ó Nualláin for his invaluable assistance with the tasks which remained.

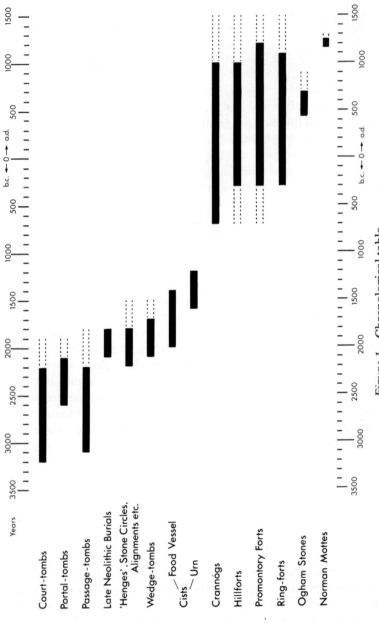

Figure 1 Chronological table

NOTE ON DATING

Radiocarbon determinations available for Ireland are as yet insufficient to permit their use as a firm chronological framework for the monuments and the episodes of Irish prehistory. Furthermore, the use of such determinations is complicated by difficulties in co-ordinating them with dates based on tree ring counts (dendrochronology). Comparison of tree ring dates with radiocarbon determinations indicates that the radiocarbon readings diverge from the tree ring dates. Dates around 1000 b.c. agree well but as we go back in time the radiocarbon 'dates' become progressively too young for several millennia while moving towards the present the opposite is the case. Thus around 4000 b.c. in real calender years the radiocarbon 'dates' may be too recent by many centuries. Current work in Ireland is throwing some light on these problems as they affect Irish dating but it is too early to attempt to apply the results. Hence, where radiocarbon determinations are quoted in the present book no attempt is made to adjust these to real calendar dates indicated by tree ring chronology.

The table (Figure 1), while taking account of radiocarbon determinations for Irish sites and comparable evidence from abroad, still depends to a large extent on sequences built up by observed associations and stratification. It is necessary to stress that the table is given as a guide for the non-specialist reader to the general sequence of the monuments and is not to be read as in any way precise or definitive. Firm lines indicate the *floruit* periods of the types while broken lines indicate probable extensions before and after. Monuments such as house sites, fences and round burial mounds which occur in many different contexts are not included. Ring-forts and Crannógs do not include possible early prototypes.

A convention using B.C. in capitals to indicate real calendar years (according to the tree ring count) and b.c. in small letters for unadjusted radiocarbon determinations is not followed in this book. The majority of dates cited are direct radiocarbon determinations or dates based on general correlations taking such determinations into account and hence b.c. and a.d. are used throughout.

MAP OF IRELAND

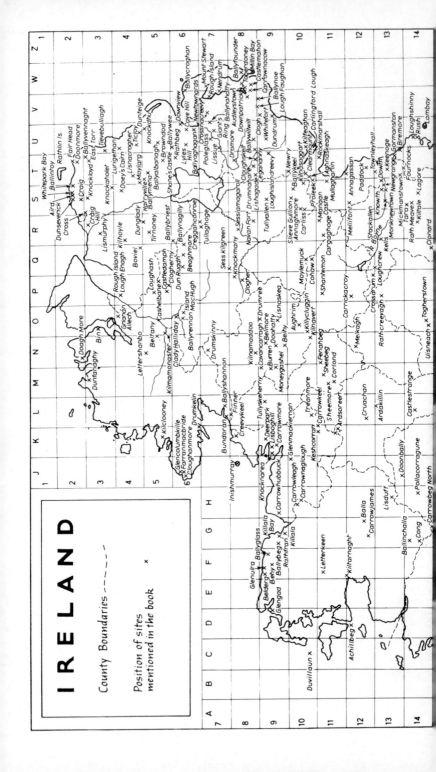

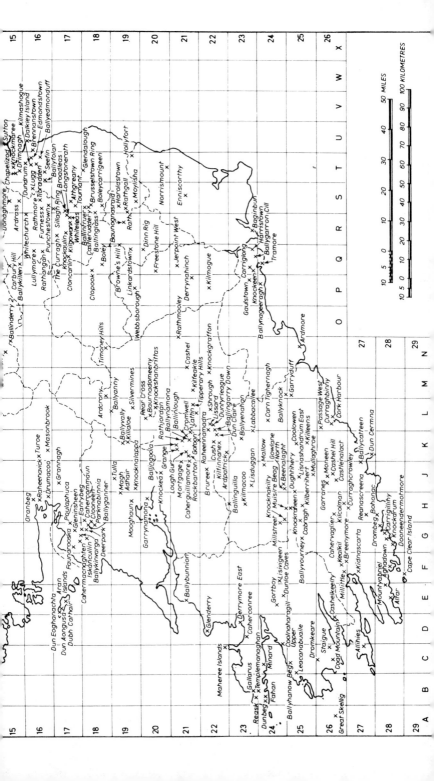

INTRODUCTION

There is no good evidence that Ireland was inhabited by man during the Old Stone (Palaeolithic) Age. After the retreat of the ice about 10,000 years ago groups of people still dependent on hunting and gathering for subsistence occupied most of northern Europe including Britain. Such Middle Stone (Mesolithic) Age people may have come to Ireland but the evidence adduced for their presence — largely flint artefacts and radiocarbon determinations — is by no means conclusive. The first New Stone (Neolithic) Age farming communities that arrived in Ireland, probably before 3000 b.c., would have found virtually if not totally virgin country. The coastal outline differed but slightly from the present one. Much of the land was heavily forested and large areas, especially in the west, were to a great extent free of the deep mountain blanket bog that now enshrouds them.

The first Neolithic colonists both in Ireland and Britain are characterized by their pottery, tools and weapons — well-made round-bottomed bowls, leaf- and lozenge-shaped flint and chert arrow-heads and polished axe-heads of flint or other suitable stone. This assemblage and the culture it represents is called Neolithic A. Many authorities believe that the long-barrow tombs which are intimately associated with the Neolithic A in both Britain and Ireland were not introduced with the earliest Neolithic colonists but were due to a later religious movement. This at first sight would seem to be supported by the fact that the bog layers providing evidence for the beginnings of land clearance and agriculture, obtained from the study of plants remains (pollen etc.), can yield radiocarbon dates earlier than those obtained from the long-barrows. However, it is clear that as soon as land clearance and agriculture was established in a district the consequential alteration in the vegetation would be expected to be represented in the bog strata, whereas the evidence from a tomb will refer to the date of its building and use. The sheer number of long-barrows extant in Ireland and Britain (over 1000) shows that the custom of long-barrow building extended over a lengthy period. Any given example may be hundreds of years later than the introduction of farming into the region in which it is situated. Indeed, since the population must have increased, the vast majority of the long-barrows should belong to times considerably later than the initial stages of colonization. In fact, evidence for date is available only for a handful of long-barrows in Ireland and Britain and some of these dates are for one reason or another suspect. With so small a sample we can hope only to gain some idea of the general period of construction of the tombs but we cannot in any wise define the earliest. The intimate and continual association of the long-barrows with the Neolithic A, combined with the absence of evidence for an alternative mode of burial, strongly favours the view that they represent the burial custom introduced with the first Neolithic A farmers. Moreover, the sheer number of bodies represented, including individuals of both sexes ranging in age from unborn children to mature adults, encourages the opinion that burial in a long-barrow was the normal right of members of the Neolithic A communities.

The earliest long-barrow builders in Ireland spread from the west, colonizing the country north of the central plain (Figure 5) and extended over to south-west Scotland and the Isle of Man. The tombs and the finds from them form a continuous province joined rather than divided by the narrow waters of the North Channel. In Britain, closely related long-barrow builders spread from the Bristol Channel region over much of southern England and southern Wales. A branch reaches into Lincolnshire and eastern Yorkshire and ultimately into eastern Scotland. Throughout all the regions occupied in both Britain and Ireland the pattern of distribution shows the settlement of the lighter well-drained soils which were relatively easily cleared and suitable for pioneering agriculture. Though exact origins on the continent cannot be isolated, features of tomb form point to western France, probably in the region around the Loire estuary.

The first farming communities altered the landscape not only by the clearance of some forest but also by the results of such clearance. Thus in Mayo there is evidence that the clearance of pine, perhaps by fire, may have encouraged the growth of blanket bog which gradually reduced even potentially fertile moraine ridges to inhospitable, heather-grown moorland. A notable feature of pollen diagrams, not only in Britain and Ireland but also in northern Europe, is the sharp decline in elm about the time of the introduction of agriculture. This is often explained as selective clearance of elm and the exploitation of the elm leaves as fodder. It is very difficult to imagine that a relatively small Neolithic population could have by mere clearance decimated the elm to the extent suggested by the pollen counts. A climatic change would be a more acceptable solution but of these there is little secure evidence. A third explanation would be the introduction of some selective tree disease. The analogy of the Dutch elm disease which has ravaged the elm over wide areas in modern times is obvious. Indeed it might be suggested that the arrival of the first farmers bringing with them livestock and seed grain, could have introduced a pest (insect, fungus or whatever) that inflicted the damage. It would not be the only time that colonists introduced parasites — all the more virulent in an area not hitherto infected.

Apart from the evidence of the settlement and way of life that the distribution of the long-barrows indicates, the artefacts found in them shed light on the economy and day-to-day life of their builders. Arrow-heads suggest hunting, serrated scrapers, perhaps the use of leather thongs, and so on. Impressions of grain on pottery tell us something of the actual crops grown, and animal bones something of the livestock. Polished stone and flint axe-heads are especially significant. They reflect one of the primary needs of these early settlers — the felling of timber whether for land clearance, house building or fuel. Some of the axes found are products of an industry for the mass production of axes. Axe factories have been discovered for example at Tievebulliagh, Co. Antrim, where veins of rock especially suitable for axe making were exploited. In such axe factories, often on high mountain slopes unsuitable for permanent habitation, the stone was chipped to the rough shape of axe-heads and brought elsewhere for final polishing. Products of such factories are found over a wide area indicating trade. In the flint districts on the chalk in England regular mines were sunk to procure good flint for axe making on a large scale. The Irish flint-bearing chalk is exposed only in the north-east along the edges of the basalt which covers the Antrim plateau. There is very considerable evidence for flint manufacture in these areas but mining on the scale of the British examples has not yet been attested.

The tombs indicate the general settlement pattern, but recent work in Co. Mayo has revealed the fields and fences of the early farmers and the furrows and ploughmarks of their tillage plots. The plans of houses at Ballyglass, Co. Mayo, and Ballynagilly, Co. Tyrone, show comfortable dwellings comparable in size to Irish rural cottages. The stout timber constructions would not merely be adequate but even quite comfortable quarters.

These long-barrow people were no mere primitive peasants let alone semi-nomadic pastoralists as has sometimes been suggested. Their farms and houses show them to have been well-organized stock raisers and agriculturalists and the axe factories imply developed industry and trade. Their fine tombs reflect not only a consummate skill in handling enormous stones but also a considerable competence in architectural design. Save for some decoration on their pottery we know little of whatever art they may have practised. A competence in navigation is implied in the sea journeys necessary not only in the initial movements from the continent but also in their diffusion to the islands of Scotland and Man. As colonists few prehistoric groups in Britain or Ireland seem to have achieved as much.

The endurance of the long-barrow tradition is no less remarkable. From among the court-tombs the portal-tombs developed. This type spread throughout the court-tomb province in the northern half of Ireland but is distinctly less common west of Sligo town where the court-tombs are very numerous (Figure 7). However, unlike the court-tombs they make a considerable impact in Leinster and Waterford and occupy the coastal fringe of Wales and extend into Cornwall. They do not appear in Scotland, though some court-tombs there have features closely akin to the portal-tomb form. Conversely some tombs assigned to the portal-tomb class in Wales have features more akin to court-tombs than to classic portal-tombs. It is perhaps worth emphasizing that the division into classes, court-tomb and portal-tomb, is one made by archeologists and we have no means of knowing to what extent these classes were considered as separate by the tomb builders. Be that as it may, the portal-tomb builders did considerably expand the long-barrow province. They had a special preference for valley-side positions near streams and an ability to penetrate along river valleys is a notable feature of their diffusion. The spread along both sides of the Irish sea shows their competence in the use of seaways. Even in Ireland itself a seaborne extension to the Waterford area and a diffusion along the Leinster river valleys is probable.

The relatively few grave goods both in Ireland and Wales show very close kinship with the court-tomb repertoire. Some finds indicate that both court-tombs and portal-tombs persisted until the dawn of the Bronze Age. We have as yet no clear indication of the stage in the Neolithic at which the portal-tomb emerged. Their numbers in Ireland are just less than half of the court-tomb total and in Donegal and central Ulster the two classes approach equality. These numbers and wide diffusion suggest a reasonably long period of currency for the portal-tombs. The overlaps in design between the two classes also implies an overlap in time between them. Less is known of the habitations of the portal-tomb than of the court-tomb builders. However, houses at Clegyr Boia in Wales may have belonged to such people.

Apart from the continuation of the use of long-barrows to the dawn of the Bronze Age the tradition represented by their pottery and flint work persists, apparently sometimes without the long-barrow. Overlaps with other cultures — passage-tomb and Early Bronze Age groups — are also indicated. One site in particular, on Knockadoon at Lough Gur, shows the retention of the classic Neolithic pottery though no proven long-barrow is known in the immediate vicinity. Some of the series of houses at Knockadoon compare in their artefacts — allowing for the poor quality of the flint available — remarkably with the long-barrows and belong to the Neolithic A tradition which continues there to overlap with Bronze Age people.

The second major element in the Irish Neolithic is represented by the passage-tombs. Like the long-barrows these derive from the great megalithic complex established along the west coast of Europe from Iberia to Scandinavia. Their precise origin is more easily defined because in the Carnac area of Brittany prototypes for their architectural features and mural art are readily identified. They represent the classic European passage-tomb, with a chamber approached by a passage under a round mound and having fine objects deposited with the burials together with an art style either depicted on the stones of the tomb or on the objects deposited. The close grouping into cemeteries and the choice of prominent sites are also features known on the continent.

The passage-tomb builders seem to have arrived in Ireland on the east coast near the Boyne estuary. They spread in strength across the northern edge of the central plain (Figure 9). This spread is marked by the four major concentrated cemeteries of Brugh na Bóinne and Loughcrew (Slieve na Calliagh) in Co. Meath and Carrowkeel and Carrowmore in Co. Sligo. From this band, possibly from Loughcrew, the tomb builders moved southwards and formed a diffused cemetery on the north-west and western fringe of the Dublin-Wicklow mountain range. Here, single cairns or small groups of two or three sites crown many of the summits. Northwards from the Boyne the movement is largely more or less coastal to north Louth and Armagh and beyond to Down and North Antrim. There is little real penetration of the heartland of the long-barrow (court-tomb and portal-tomb) and the relatively few sites in Tyrone, Fermanagh and Donegal tend to fall in areas not densely occupied by long-barrow tombs. At first sight the penetration in Sligo seems to indicate a considerable overlap between the two series but it is noteworthy that this penetration is along a corridor in which the court-tombs and portal-tombs are distinctly few by comparison with the great densities found on either side. In Leinster also the portal-tombs lie rather to the north of the Dublin-Wicklow massif in contrast to the more western aspect of the passage-tombs. The riverine distribution of portal-tombs in the valleys of the rivers opening to Waterford and Wexford estuaries shows but a slight overlap with the passage-tombs, save for the tiny Tramore group of undifferentiated passage-tombs which are probably considerably later than the main passage-tomb series. In common with the court-tombs and portal-tombs, passage-tombs are scarcely represented in the south-west of Ireland.

The specific siting of passage-tombs and the general cemetery pattern make the tracing of the actual lands occupied by their builders less easy than in the case of the other Irish megalithic tomb builders. One important factor has been noted — a general association with glacial gravel terrain. The Boyne area is largely such land. The Dublin-Wicklow sites overlook glacial gravels on the rim of the plain and the corridor overlooked by the Sligo series is also rolling moraine land. Carrowmore itself is built on glacial sands and gravel. Though a full detailed survey of the lands overlooked by the tombs has yet to be completed it is likely to show a distinct association with glacial gravels over most if not all the regions occupied. The passage-tombs, then, display not only a considerable degree of mutual exclusiveness in the general territory occupied but also a choice of land different from the soils selected by the court-tomb and portal-tomb builders. In their relation to more or less lowland glacial gravels and sands the passage-tombs accord more with the choice of Food Vessel people of the Early Bronze Age. The presence of a group on the headlands of North Antrim in a flint-rich chalk area and also near the axe factory on Rathlin Island suggests that they, like their court-tomb contemporaries, had an interest in the mass production of axes which is a marked feature of the Neolithic in Ireland and Britain.

In dealing with the finds from passage-tombs another contrast is apparent. In a number of Irish passage-tombs complete undisturbed burial deposits have been found, while such deposits are scarcely available from other Irish megalithic tombs. The better preservation in passage-tombs is due partly to the more complete coverage of the chambers within the round mounds which envelop them and partly to the more remote hill-top siting of many of them. In well-preserved deposits a thick layer of cremated bones, representing a large number of individuals, has been found and with them a very standard assemblage of grave goods: beads, pendants, bone pins, stone and clay balls and pottery. The emphasis is on personal ornament, and practical tools and weapons are seldom present in the actual burial deposit though these may occur elsewhere in the mound. The pottery consists of round-bottomed hemispherical bowls rather coarse in texture and decorated in stabs. In manufacture it compares none too favourably with the finer wares of the court-tombs but the designs, looped arcs, etc., more obviously reflect the traditional megalithic art associated with passage-tombs throughout their continental distribution. The ornaments found, though differing in detail, accord with the finds of beads and decorated objects in the tombs of France and Iberia. Moreover, though non-utilitarian in nature they to some extent reflect tools such as pestle hammers which were presumably part of the passage-tomb builders' equipment.

The mural engravings on the tombs which are a notable feature, except in the west of Ireland, give us an insight into the artistic achievement of the tomb builders. In Iberia this art is reflected in ornamented stone and bone objects placed in the tombs, together with the remains of painted designs and a few engravings on the walls. In Brittany elaborate wall engravings are well represented. The finest Irish art is in the Boyne region especially in the greatest of the tombs Newgrange, Dowth and Knowth.

We have but little knowledge of the houses of the Irish passage-tomb builders. Layers of habitation refuse under some mounds, e.g. Townleyhall, may be due merely to temporary squatting perhaps by the tomb builders. It has been suggested that the very size of the tombs and the organization required for their construction together with their cemetery siting imply close-knit communities and even towns. The art and the emphasis on ornament is taken as showing advancement consistent with such communities. In support of this townships associated with passage-tomb cemeteries such as at Los Millares in Iberia can be cited. In Ireland, however, unless the hut circles on Carrowkeel are accepted, there is no direct evidence.

It is true that the finest of the Irish passage-tombs exceed in the sheer quantity of material used (about 100,000 tonnes in the largest examples) and in architectural excellence even the greatest of the long-barrow tombs of Ireland. It must be remembered, however, that the number of these giants is very few compared with the total number of Irish passage-tombs. The three great tumuli on the Boyne about 80 m in diameter, the great cairns at Knocknarea and Heapstown about 60 m in diameter and cairn D at Loughcrew 54 m, are exceptional rather than representative of the series. In fact the vast majority of the Irish passage-tombs would accord in their architectural achievement and even in sheer weight of material used with the court-tomb series and a considerable number of them are puny compared even with normal court-tombs or portal-tombs.

The number of bodies represented in well-preserved passage-tomb burial deposits is larger than those found in long-barrows either in Ireland or Britain. Thus, even allowing for the greater degree of disturbance normally present in Irish court-tombs and portal-tombs and the frequency of acid soil conditions, each passage-tomb is likely to represent a larger number of people than would a tomb of the long-barrow class. This should mean either that a passage-tomb served a more numerous community than did tombs of the other classes or that it was used over a longer period.

The total number of passage-tombs recognized in Ireland is less easy to define than that of the other classes of megalithic tombs largely because it is often impossible to decide from surface evidence whether a round mound contains a passage-tomb or burials of other types. However, a figure of about 300 would be generally acceptable. About 500 long-barrow tombs (court-tombs and portal-tombs) are attested in Ireland. The overall total of 800 is, of course, considerably less than the number actually constructed because past destruction and future recognition must be allowed for. There are too many imponderables to permit any precise estimate of the proportion of the Neolithic population accounted for in these burials but it seems possible to infer that the numbers are sufficiently high to rule out the assumption that megalithic burial was confined to a small upper stratum in the societies.

The presence of cemeteries shows a tendency to centralize burials but this need not necessarily imply concentrated settlement. The diffused cemeteries like those in the Dublin-Wicklow region and in Antrim suggest considerable travel to the burial ground, and rural communities could easily account for them. Even in the Boyne region, including the great examples, rural communities on the rich pasture and arable land could probably have accomplished the task of building them over a number of years. What is implied in the greatest of the tombs is an impelling motivation probably controlled by rich and powerful leadership. The passage-tombs of Ireland then may perhaps reflect some more or less urban tradition in the background in Iberia but it is very doubtful if they formed urban settlements as such in Ireland. Many great monuments — such as hill-forts — were built in Ireland long before the Vikings first established urban life here.

The date of arrival of the passage-tombs is usually taken to be about 2500 b.c., several hundreds of years after the arrival of the long-barrow. However, there are certain factors, e.g. the presence of transeptal sites in both classes, that make too wide a separation in time for the beginnings of each somewhat difficult to sustain. The relatively confined spread of passage-tombs in Ireland and even more so in Britain suggests that the long-barrow people continued to flourish side by side with the passage-tomb builders. In any case both types seem to have persisted into the dawn of the Bronze Age. Contacts between the two are suggested by the occasional occurrence of passage-tomb pottery (Carrowkeel ware) in court-tombs as at Audleystown, Co. Down and Neolithic A ware in passage-tomb sites such as 'The Druid Stone' at Ballintoy, Co. Antrim.

Like the court-tombs and the main long-barrow series in southern Britain the passage-tombs in Ireland imply the arrival of a sizeable group of immigrants. The culture represented by them includes not merely novel architecture, art and grave goods, but also a coherent pattern in the siting of tombs. The choice of settlement areas suggests economic requirements differing to a degree from those of the court-tomb builders. These can scarcely be accounted for by the arrival of mere missionaries, traders or casual contacts. The size of the immigrant group capable of establishing the culture is quite impossible to define and guesses could range from as few as a hundred to many times that number.

Over much of western Europe the spread of metalworking is associated with people who used a special form of decorated pottery known as Beaker. The characteristic burial mode of these people was individual inhumation and their equipment included barbed-and-tanged flint arrow-heads and archers' wristguards. Along much of the western coastlands of Europe megalithic tomb builders were still present at the dawn of the Bronze Age and the general condition in these areas is one both of change due to the new Bronze Age elements and also of a degree of continuity of the older usages. The Early Irish Bronze Age comprises several new groups. Each can be seen to a greater or lesser degree as emerging from the Beaker tradition with its custom of individual interment combining with the older megalithic collective burial tradition. Five episodes can be distinguished, each with its characteristic monument, as follows: Late Neolithic single burials, Wedge tombs; Food Vessel burials; stone circles and embanked enclosures. It is not as yet possible to arrange the beginnings of these in any strict chronological sequence and in any case a considerable overlap between most of them is very likely. It must suffice to say that the Irish Bronze Age began probably a century or two before 2000 b.c. and that the duration of the customs established by the major movements extended to 1500 b.c. and perhaps even later. Since our knowledge of the wedge-tomb and the Food Vessel is fuller than those of the other episodes and since these two are the most widespread, it is convenient to deal with them first, always remembering that the order of treatment does not imply a chronological sequence for the beginnings of each.

Convincing prototypes of the wedge-tombs and their grave goods (Beaker, coarse ware, barbed-and-tanged arrow-heads) are to be found in the very similar tombs widespread on the Breton peninsula of north-west France. These tombs represent the continuance of the old megalithic collective burial tradition joined by customs derived from the metalworking Beaker-using people. Wedge-tombs have a markedly western distribution in Ireland (Figure 11) and they belong to the first great colonizers of west Munster as yet recognized. Their distribution on the peninsulas of Cork and Kerry bears a distinct relationship to the rich copper deposits there which are known to have been worked in Bronze Age times. A concentration on the hills on either side of the Shannon in Tipperary and east Clare probably also represents an early focus around the rich copper districts and from here emerges a movement in strength northwards to north Connaught and across central Ulster. The general adherence throughout to light rather upland soils suggests an emphasis on pasturage, particularly apparent in the great density on the Burren plateau of Clare. The penetration of north Connaught and central Ulster takes over as it were much of the heartland of the court-tomb builders. The distinct weakness in the east is probably largely due to the presence of the Food Vessel people. We know far too little of the burial deposits in the tombs to guess at the number of individuals interred in each save that collective burial is certainly attested. The little skeletal material that we do have suggests that a round-headed strain (characteristic of Beaker-using people), as distinct from the long-headed Neolithic type, is present.

The spread of the Food Vessel people indicated by their burials is in sharp contrast to that of the wedge-tomb builders. The weight is distinctly in the east and a clear preference for sandy esker soils is apparent. Two major types of Food Vessel are recognized — Bowl Food Vessel and Vase Food Vessel. In the case of the Bowl type unburned, usually crouched, burials occur in about equal numbers to those with cremation whereas with the Vase type cremation is virtually the constant rite. The crouched burial is the normal Beaker rite and the decoration on Food Vessels owes much to that of the Beakers. The exact origin of the Food Vessel is not certainly known but some Dutch Beakers (Veluwe type) come quite close to the Food Vessel form. It would appear that a movement from the Netherlands crossed northern England and southern Scotland into Ireland probably across the North Channel. In doing so it would be open to influences not only from contemporary standard Beaker users but also from Neolithic survivors in the region.

The territory occupied by the Food Vessel people is complementary to that of the wedge-tomb builders (compare Figures 11 and 12) and between the two series virtually every district in Ireland, save for the more inhospitable mountain regions is penetrated. Both represent sizeable colonizations which flourished side by side for a long period. Overlap between the two series is found in so far as some wedge-tombs contain Food Vessel as well as Beaker and, in the east, the cairn of a wedge-tomb at Kilmashogue, Co. Dublin, was apparently enlarged to receive Food Vessel burial. Specific contact with passage-tombs, though not necessarily with their builders, is indicated by the re-use of several of them as cemetery mounds by Food Vessel users. It is possible that the preference for prominent siting which many cemetery mounds share with passage-tombs betrays an influence from passage-tomb custom. On the other hand it may well be that such a preference is an integral part of the Food Vessel cemetery-cairn tradition and that the round hill-top passage-tomb mound was chosen because its siting served this preference. In some cases at least a very clear dichotomy between the two cultures is indicated by the scant respect shown to passage-tomb interments, as was so in the Mound of the Hostages at Tara. On the other hand cemetery cairns were sometimes built in close juxtaposition to passage-tombs hinting perhaps at a certain continuity of tradition. Another hint at such a continuity is given by the presence of massive cists of nearly megalithic proportions as the central element in cemetery mounds.

A closely integrated stone-circle complex with alignments, standing stones, boulder burials and cairns has been recently isolated in west Cork and Kerry. By comparison with the wedge-tombs and Food Vessels the territory covered is small. Like the wedge-tombs an interest in copper is shown by the occurrence of many in copper-bearing areas. Little direct evidence of dating is as yet available but the few objects known accord with the general Beaker context indicated by the finds from stone circles elsewhere in Britain and Ireland. The inheritance of megalithic traditions is shown by the use of large stones and in particular by the boulder burials, the heavy covers of which are reminiscent of the small simple tombs of the passage-tomb family. The evidence for burial from the few examples excavated points to a cremation covered by the boulder cover or, if no boulder structure exists, in a pit more or less centrally placed in the circle.

The distribution of this stone-circle complex *vis-à-vis* that of the wedge-tombs is not inconsistent with contemporaneity. It is worth noting that both stone circle and wedge-tomb adhere constantly to a roughly north-east-south-west axis of direction. While orientation bias is known from other series, e.g. court-tombs, the constancy of adherence to the rule is shared only by the southern stone-circle group and the wedge-tombs. It is probably more than a coincidence and hints at a common tradition.

The origin of the Cork-Kerry series is as yet uncertain. However, Brittany once again offers the best source because there a large number of free-standing megalithic monuments, alignments, standing stones and perhaps a few stone circles are found. In south-west England alignments and circles are known and these may point to the immediate place of origin for the south-western group in Ireland. If links between these areas were established the rich copper ores of the south-west would be brought together with the tin of Cornwall and Brittany. In passing it may be noted that such a connection would be paralleled by the links between the Scilly-Cornwall group of late passage-tombs with the little group of closely similar tombs in the Tramore area of Waterford, which like the south-west of Ireland is rich in copper.

Stone-circle groups elsewhere in Ireland (Figure 15) such as the numerous mid-Ulster group are more difficult to place in context. It is scarcely possible to explain them as offshoots of the Cork-Kerry series. Little can be said as yet save that such dating evidence as does exist would not forbid a date early in the second millennium b.c.

In recent years evidence for an intrusion of Beaker-using people has been discovered in eastern Ireland. In the Boyne area on the skirts of the great passage-tomb tumuli of Knowth and Newgrange considerable activity by Beaker-users is present. This seems to be the context of the great freestanding stone circle around Newgrange. At Monknewtown an embanked enclosure also showed strong Beaker connections and enclosures in the general Boyne area may prove to belong to the same context. Outside the Boyne region the great embanked enclosure of 'The Giant's Ring' at Ballynahally near Belfast, again demonstrates the connection. Such a connection is vividly brought out by the occurrence of a single cremated burial accompanied by a pot of passage-grave style within the enclosure at Monknewtown. The evidence to date accords with a suggestion that Beaker-using people who practised the custom of building these enclosures, usually known as henge monuments, were attracted to the great passage-tomb centres of eastern Ireland. This henge tradition is reflected not only by the embanked enclosures but also by the presence of free-standing stone circles around Newgrange and occasionally elsewhere, e.g. Millin Bay and Ballynoe, Co. Down. The function of the embanked enclosures is not clear. Their design suggests an inward-looking amphitheatre rather than any defensive function.

One site outside the eastern passage-tomb area, the great embanked stone circle at Grange, Co. Limerick, seems to reflect the same tradition. Beaker finds confirm its cultural and chronological context. How far the other stone circles in the vicinity are also related remains as yet unclear.

A distinctive episode at the dawn of the Bronze Age is represented by a small group of specialized single burials in the Leinster region. These have been assigned to the Neolithic partly on the basis of the specialized 'hanging-bowl' pottery that accompanies the single inhumation and partly because, in some instances, pottery in the Neolithic A tradition was found. Several theories have been advanced to explain these burials. Direct foreign influence has been put forward by one authority while others have suggested derivation from Irish sources. It is possible to argue passage-tomb connections from the heavy, partly corbelled cists, the mound form, and the tendency to prominent siting but to a degree at least, some Food Vessel type burials, especially perhaps those with Bowl Food Vessels, share these features. What is certain is that the specialized pottery has also been found in both portal-tombs and court-tombs. Some traits of the pottery suggest relationships with the so-called Beacharra wares of court-tombs while others seem closer to the Bowl Food Vessel style.

If passage-tomb influences are present these need not derive from the Irish series because the passage-tomb tradition is strong over much of Atlantic Europe from Spain to Denmark and Sweden. Indeed in Brittany little corbelled cists known as *coffres* occur in association with simple passage-tomb forms at the great long mound of Mont St Michel at Carnac. Such *coffres* are also known from long mounds at Manio and at the stone circles of Er-Lannic. The associated pottery is a specialized fine form known as vase-supports which are decorated in a style strongly reminiscent of passage-tomb art. While this need not at all imply any direct connection with the Irish single burials it may well indicate parallel developments.

In the complex situation that existed in eastern Ireland around 2000 b.c. some mixing and overlap of traditions is very likely. Be that as it may, even if the exact explanation of the Irish sites eludes us they can be accepted as another instance of the single burial tradition superseding the older collective megalithic mode while borrowing some features from it.

At the outset of this section it was pointed out that it was difficult to place the beginnings of these episodes in chronological order. Overlap with existing Neolithic A or passage-tomb pottery can be cited for all groups, though this is rather tenuous in the case of the Food Vessel, but this alone is insufficient to determine a sequence because in some places the older traditions may have had a long survival. It could be argued, of course, that those which reflect the normal Beaker should be earliest but once again the different conditions in different parts of the country complicate the picture — for instance, the eastern arrivals will be confronted by well-established Neolithic usages while the earliest Bronze Age intruders in the south-west may well have made their initial settlements free of any influence from established communities.

The great strength of the Irish Early Bronze Age is seen in its products in bronze and gold and in its far-flung exports of such objects as gold lunulae and decorated bronze axes. This apparent wealth arose not only from the rich metal resources exploited by the inhabitants but also from the opening up and cultivation of so much of the land. It is difficult to assess precisely the part played by each group but much of the credit must go to the Food Vessel people whose connections with northern Britain and so across to the continent were implicit in their origins. It would appear that throughout the ensuing Bronze Age the old Atlantic route, so dominant in the preceding stages, became less important than the connections eastward to Britain and northern Europe.

About the middle of the second millennium b.c. a new custom of burial was brought to Ireland from Britain. This consisted of individual cremated burial within an upturned Cinerary Urn. The practice spread initially into the north-east of the country and soon mingled with that of the Food Vessel people, covering most of the territory occupied by them (Figure 13). Already in Britain an overlap in the Urn and Food Vessel is present and though separate strands within the Urn tradition can be recognized, on the basis of pottery form and to an extent in distribution and accompanying grave goods, the whole series shows a general unity. Two of the four classes of Cinerary Urn (Encrusted and Enlarged Food Vessel) show the clearest interaction with Food Vessel while the other two (Collared and Cordoned) appear to be less affected. However, the frequent occurrence of all Urn types in cemeteries which also contain Food Vessel burials, in several cases sharing the one grave, indicates the existence side by side of both the Food Vessel and Urn mode of burial and for the most part it seems best to regard the two traditions as intermixing into what may be regarded as the one society. It is notable that it is with the Vase Food Vessel that the associations with Cinerary Urns occur and the dominance of the cremation rite with these, in comparison with the 50 per cent of inhumations with the Bowl Food Vessel, may be to some extent influenced by the constant cremation tradition of the Cinerary Urn. In the close association of the Food Vessel and Urn certain trends can be discerned. With the Urn the custom of cist burial declines. Many Urns are unprotected by cists and the cists themselves tend to be protective coverings for the Urns rather than the stone box-type cist normal with burials accompanied by Food Vessel. Flat cemeteries are favoured to a greater extent by Urn users than by those of Food Vessel and in most cases when Urns are found in cemetery mounds they share the mound with Food Vessels. A small group of Cordoned Urn burials in the west of Ireland contain a primary central Cordoned Urn without any Food Vessel. There is some evidence also that some Urn burials at least used mounds with fosses sometimes approaching the ring-barrow form.

It is difficult, if not indeed impossible, to explain the introduction of the Food Vessel burials without allowing a sizeable incursion of people. In the case of the Urn, while it undoubtedly represented the spread of a new burial site into the Food Vessel region of north Britain and Ireland, it may not be necessary to envisage any great influx of new people into Ireland. With the new burial modes other fashions, e.g. bronze razors, were undoubtedly introduced. Contacts percolating throughout the whole British-Irish zone through trade or other travel could possibly account for the phenomenon. Even so the Urn burials represent a notable episode in the middle of the Irish Bronze Age. The spread of the Urn tradition and also of the Food Vessel particularly of the Vase type shows once again that the North Channel unites rather than divides a cultural region straddling its narrow waters.

Very few field monuments can be assigned to the later Bronze Age. The burial record closes with the Cinerary Urn burials probably about 1200 b.c. For several centuries thereafter no habitations have been recognized, pottery is unknown and our knowledge must depend very largely on metalwork.

Important developments in the metal industry are evident in the twelfth century b.c. These distinguish the Bishopsland Phase called after a hoard found in the townland of that name in County Kildare. In this phase new specialist crafts such as the use of clay moulds for casting and certain new types of tools and ornament are introduced. Some of the products are of the highest standard of workmanship, e.g. bronze rapiers and gold torcs. There are also clear indications of the continuance of metal types current in the preceding period. Thus the Bishopsland Phase might be described as the product of the earlier tradition in metalwork combined with a new expertise and new designs. The emphasis on craftsmanship is reflected in the tools found in the hoards and in the presence in some of unfinished gold objects.

In theory at least, immigrant craftsmen could have brought about the changes apparent in the Bishopsland Phase, but the loss of the burial record, previously so well represented, suggests a more deep-rooted change requiring a more substantial incursion of people to explain it. Yet the apparent change in the burial record may be less extreme than may at first sight appear. In both Food Vessel and Cinerary Urn contexts simple cremations without accompanying or covering pots occur. It is clear that such burials were at least countenanced. After the use of sepulchral vessels ceased, such simple cremations could well have become the normal practice. Unless some durable and dateable objects accompanied simple cremations we would remain in ignorance as to their date. Many Urn burials have no grave goods other than the covering vessel and in these circumstances a corresponding paucity of grave goods with simple cremations would be expected. It is possible that some mounds which produced no pots but only simple cremations in pits belong to the period after 1200 b.c. The same would be true of flat cemeteries and isolated burials and indeed these might well escape notice completely. Such a theory, and it must be emphasized that it is only a theory at present, would not only explain the paucity of the record but would also make any sizeable intrusion of new people in the Bishopsland Phase an unnecessary assumption.

The changes in the metalwork in the Bishopsland Phase hint at influences from several sources but connections with south Britain seem to be dominant. Some export from Ireland is also probable. Following the Bishopsland Phase from about 1000 b.c. some new influences appear — notably the introduction of the first true swords. Contacts with Britain, at least northern Britain, are maintained but there is little sign of any major new arrivals. The dearth of material suggests perhaps that this was a time of no great development.

About 700 b.c. radical changes in the metalwork are evident. A whole range of new types, trumpets, cauldrons etc. in bronze, together with a wealth of gold ornaments including magnificent gorgets and 'lock-rings' appear. The craftsmanship is superb and the sheer wealth, e.g. the Great Clare Gold Hoard, is astonishing. The bronze work includes complex castings and lead is a notable component in the alloy used. Two major provinces have been recognized on the basis of the metalwork — one in north Munster and the other in the north-east of the country. The wealth of the north Munster group probably derives not only from the exploitation of the rich lowlands of central Munster (including the Golden Vein) but also from the rich metal (copper and lead) on either side of the Shannon as in the Silvermines district in County Tipperary and the Tulla region of Clare. The foreign connections of the north Munster group which is centred on the lower Shannon with its wide estuary are complex, with evident contacts along the old Atlantic route towards France and Iberia and others pointing to the west Baltic. The north-eastern group shares several features with that of north Munster. However, its distribution suggests contacts across the north Channel with Britain and beyond to the Nordic lands.

This period in the Bronze Age is called the Dowris Phase from a place in County Offaly where a rich and varied hoard of metalwork was discovered in the last century. The principal types of settlement site known to belong to this period are lake-dwellings at Ballinderry No. 2, Co. Offaly; Knocknalappa, Co. Clare; and Rathtinaun, Co. Sligo. These crannógs are platforms constructed near the lake edge. As is discussed in a later chapter, crannógs are an important type of settlement side by side with ring-forts in the first millennium a.d. It seems likely that the custom of lake-dwelling was introduced in the Dowris Phase and was adopted and adapted by the later Iron Age people who established the ring-fort as the standard farmstead.

The rôle of the Shannon basin in the Dowris Phase appears particularly important both for the highway it could provide and the rich alluvial soils which, apparently for the first time, were widely exploited. A detailed study of the distribution of sites and finds from this phase would probably show that the great basins of the Bann and Lough Neagh system play a rôle in the northern zone. It is of some interest that dugout canoes suitable for lake and river travel have been found associated with this phase. Trade connections to Britain are suggested by finds from there and these imply the presence of seagoing craft.

Besides crannóg-type habitations it may be that some hill-forts were constructed in the Dowris Phase. At Rathgall, Co. Wicklow, intensive activity of people belonging to this time was revealed by excavations within a large multivallate hill-fort. Future excavation must determine the relations of this activity to the ramparts. The position of the huge multivallate hill-fort at Mooghaun, Co. Clare, overlooking the Fergus, a tributary of the Shannon, together with the discovery about half a mile away of the Great Clare Gold Hoard hints at a possibility that this site also may have been occupied in Late Bronze Age times. Hill-fort building in the Late Bronze Age is attested in Britain and this makes the occurrence of such in Ireland a reasonable possibility. However, pending verification by excavation it remains a possibility only.

At Rathgall the first burial assigned to the Late Bronze Age has recently been reported. This was a cremation burial with a large bucket-shaped pottery vessel. Unlike the normal Cinerary Urn burials of earlier times the pot was upright. Pottery is attested at several sites, Knocknalappa, Ballinderry No. 2. This pottery is flat-bottomed, bucket-shaped ware and some examples are necked below the rim in a manner reminiscent of the bronze buckets of the period.

The great technological changes and the wealth of new types together with the new distribution pattern suggest an influx of new people. When the general lowland aspect of the distribution, the use of waterways and especially the lake-dwellings are considered it seems likely that a source should be sought in low, well-watered land. Some of the types such as buckets and cauldrons show densities along the Thames and other rivers in eastern England, suggesting also a riverine pattern. It is far too early to place any great weight on such considerations. It must also be emphasized that though there is a sufficient degree of unity in the Dowris Phase to allow it to be treated as a coherent whole, certain more localized contacts and influences, such as those apparent across the North Channel, must be taken into account.

By this time Celtic-speaking people are known to have been established on the continent. It is possible, therefore, that the people who introduced the Dowris Phase were likewise Celtic-speaking. The use of lake-dwellings might give an indication of the origin of these people. There is an interesting passage in the Greek author, Strabo, writing about the beginning of the Christian era referring to Celtic tribes in the Ardennes region who 'had small islands in the marshes' to which they retreated when attacked. This, of course, is far too late to have any direct relevance to the crannógs of the Dowris Phase but it does indicate that lake-dwellings, whether on natural or artificial islands is not clear, were used by some Celtic people on the continent in the last century b.c. How far this custom extends to earlier times is unknown.

The chronology of the end of the Bronze Age and the beginning of the Early Iron Age in Ireland is notoriously difficult. It must suffice to say that the transition took place in the latter half of the first millennium b.c. The number of actual monuments that can with certainty be dated to the pagan Iron Age in Ireland is limited, but it is clear that several classes were well established in this time, hill-forts, ring-forts and crannógs, and that over part of the country a considerable number of artefacts — mainly distinguished by their art style (La Tène) — represent an important episode. Little in the nature of real history is known before Christianity was established in the fifth century a.d. but some admittedly uncertain light is thrown on the period from the tales and traditions committed to writing some centuries later.

Recent advances in the study of the Iron Age have shown that two distinct cultural elements are present and a third can be less clearly defined. The objects belonging to the La Tène are largely confined to the northern half of the country. They include works in metal such as scabbards, horse-bits and brooches decorated with the typical style and decorated stones such as that at Turoe, Co. Galway. The most numerous objects represented are beehive querns. None of this material is clearly associated with ring-forts. Some La Tène connection seems probable at Emain Macha (Navam Fort) hill-fort and a site, at Lisnacrogher, Co. Antrim, which may have been a crannóg yielded very rich finds belonging to the La Tène group. The connections of Irish La Tène with northern England and Scotland are clear and it would appear that once again in prehistory the North Channel links rather than divides.

The second great element in the Irish Iron Age is intimately associated with the great ring-fort tradition which becomes so dominant throughout all Ireland in the first millennium a.d. and persists for centuries thereafter. The type of quern associated with this element is of disc form and the La Tène ornament is absent. The duality of the Irish Iron Age is further demonstrated by the two types of hill-fort. The univallate type is dominant in the north while the multivallate type is best represented in the south and west. To an extent the Leinster region disturbs a simple division into a northern and a southern zone. In the Wicklow area the multivallate hill-fort impinges on the area where the univallate type is also known. Furthermore features such as the internal fosse and elaborate ritual enclosures link Dún Ailinne, the ancient seat of the kings of Leinster, with the royal site of Meath at Tara and that of Ulster at Emain Macha.

The archaeological evidence suggests an incursion into the northern half of Ireland by La Tène people. This is often taken as representing the arrival of a warrior class though the numerous beehive querns might perhaps suggest some colonization of a more general nature. The multivallate hill-forts and the stone ring-forts which seem to belong to the same context can be interpreted as representing the arrival in the west of Ireland of a different Iron Age people who were outside the La Tène tradition. The most likely origin for these is to the south along the old Atlantic route and certain analogies between Iberian forts and both the multivallate hill-forts and the stone ring-forts could be cited. Iberia was at this time largely Celtic and the La Tène culture did not spread into it. The linguistic evidence from the Celtic inscriptions is tenuous but there are hints that the Celtic language in Iberia was of the Q-Celtic form to which the Irish language belongs. It would be possible to suggest that the great forts in Aran and others in Clare and Kerry, which are very difficult to accept as last-ditch defences of a retreating people as has sometimes been claimed, were more in the nature of bridgehead fortifications built in the early stages of conquest.

The Leinster position sharing as it does something of the northern features could be due to contacts across the Irish sea, analogous but not identical with the clear La Tène intrusion across the North Channel.

The general historical setting in Ireland fits the general picture deduced from the archaeological evidence. The ancient province of Ulster extended over much of the north of Ireland and reached to the Boyne. Then the Connaught power expanded. It encroached on the north-west of Ulster leading to the formation of the kingdom of Ailech — whose capital seems to have been a multivallate hill-fort at Ailech in Donegal. Central Ulster became Airghialla and the ancient Ulaid having lost Emain Macha survived east of the Bann with a capital at Downpatrick. Meanwhile the Connaught dynasties had taken over much of the midlands including the royal site of Tara. Leinster, though under pressure and tribute, remains to some degree unconquered and frequently in historic times plays a rôle apart. In the expansion of Connaught power Munster remains more or less aloof. The historical sources for this general state of affairs date to many centuries after the Iron Age incursions suggested by archeological evidence but may well reflect events initiated by them.

The historical record shows that during the Roman occupation of Britain the Irish took part in raids on Roman territories and finds of Roman silver in Ireland bear witness to this. Colonial settlement from the north-east of Ireland into south-west Scotland were well under way in the fifth century a.d. and ultimately spread the Gaelic language over the greater part of Scotland. In the middle of the ninth century a.d. the Irish and Pictish dynasties were united bringing most of Scotland under one rule. There were also in the early centuries of the Christian era settlements of Leinstermen in Wales where the name of the Lleyn peninsula commemorates their presence. People from the Waterford and east Cork area occupied districts in south Wales and Cornwall.

The Iron Age shows many features paralleled in earlier times. A movement from the south from Atlantic Europe impinging initially on western Ireland seems to be probable and there is clear evidence for an intrusion from Britain across the North Channel into the north of Ireland. Some intrusion into Leinster from western Britain is also probable. On the other hand expansions from Ireland into western Scotland and the Isle of Man and from Leinster and south-east Munster into Wales and Cornwall are known. All these movements find counterparts in earlier times. The chronology of the monuments and the finds related to them is not as yet sufficiently clear to verify or correct the historical data, but the picture that is slowly emerging suggests that future work will allow a closer co-ordination between the two sources of evidence.

The sagas also help to support the general picture. The classic tale of Táin Bó Cuailgne reflects a conflict between the Connaught forces and Ulster. It may be significant that a Leinster group, the Galeóin, while allies of Connaught, were obviously not entirely trusted and were scattered among the Connaught armies rather than moving as a unit. The story of Togail Bruidne Dá Derga perhaps reflects a separate Leinster episode from a base in Britain. Though these tales are doubtless largely legendary they do seem to reflect happenings in Ireland before the dawn of reliable historical record.

The extent to which the formation of Early Iron Age Ireland is due to a considerable influx of people can be assessed on two grounds, firstly the implantation of the Irish language and secondly the extent to which large cultural changes are evident. The implantation of a new language without organized general education can hardly be explained without a sizeable immigrant population. The standardization of the ring-fort type settlement and the whole range of new Iron Age objects also favour this. It is on general grounds probable that the La Téne people of northern Britain were Brythonic rather than Gaelic in speech but efforts to demonstrate any significant Brythonic element in Ireland in the pagan Iron Age have not been convincing. If they were, and if they succeeded in implanting their language, it was submerged in the Gaelic tradition before Christian times. Because of the eventual dominance of the ring-fort tradition and its culture over all Ireland it seems most probable that its bearers were the major

Celtic conquerors of the land. The crannógs introduced by the Late Bronze Age Dowris people were adopted by the ring-fort builders and the features both of structure and of context that are common between the two types in the succeeding centuries could be taken to reflect the adaptation of the earlier tradition. In connection with the Dowris Phase it could be suggested that the position of Munster, aloof from the main conflict, was in some measure due to the strength of the Dowris people there. We have noticed before that the Dowris people could have been Celtic but one tiny shred of evidence perhaps tends to hint otherwise. The Old Irish name for Munster, *Mumu*, differs from the normal names current in Early Celtic Ireland and may itself be pre-Celtic.

The basis social structure of Ireland as reflected in the archaeology, particularly in the ring-fort, scarcely changes with the introduction of Christianity in the fifth century a.d. Material closely dateable to the fifth and sixth centuries is not abundant. However, some ecclesiastical sites are known to have been founded but though there is historical evidence, for instance, of wooden churches of this period, we know very little of their form from archaeological sources. It is very likely also that clochán-type cells and small oratories were also constructed. The cillín sites probably have a long range in date but how soon such enclosures were begun to be used is not clear. Some slabs inscribed with crosses should go back also to this time. Many ogham stones certainly do. Some authorities would place their beginning before the Patrician mission from 432 a.d. Their context appears distinctly Christian and they may well represent a Christian society established independently and perhaps very shortly before the arrival of St Patrick in 432 a.d. The connection with Wales and Cornwall is clear. Munster colonizers in these areas are recorded and they or the other Irish settlers in western Britain from Leinster might be responsible. Whatever the detail may be the ogham stones prove a direct connection between the Munster region and south-west Britain.

The later Christian monuments, churches, round towers, high crosses etc. are outside the scope of this work. These, however, like the earlier monuments can be seen to mark notable episodes in church history, and the distribution of several can be linked with geographical and political regions. The spread of Christianity from Ireland first to Iona with Columcille in 563 a.d. and on into Scotland and Northumbria is reflected in cross-slabs and the development of the high cross is linked with it. Indeed the spread of Christianity to Northumbria, analogous to the many previous connections noted across the North Channel, played a significant rôle in the development of the great flowering of Irish art about 700 a.d. In this art the old Celtic La Tène tradition combines with influences from Roman and Anglo-Saxon art together with Coptic elements. Such masterpieces of Irish art as the Ardagh Chalice, the Book of Durrow and the Tara Brooch owe much to the close contact within the Celtic Church on both sides of the Channel.

The Viking raids led to the establishment of settlements in centres like Dublin, Limerick and Waterford which later grew into towns. Elsewhere some graves and finds are known though not unnaturally much of the booty is found in the Norwegian homeland. The raids may well have encouraged the building of round towers as a protective measure. Scandinavian influence on Irish art is apparent especially after the defeat of the Vikings and their acceptance of Christianity in the early eleventh century. The coming of Romanesque in the early twelfth century reflects the contacts with the continent, with the Malachy reforms and the establishment of the Norman monasteries of the regular orders, e.g. the Cistercian foundation of Mellifont, Co. Louth, reflecting a new phase in Irish Church history. This is followed by the Normans whose very initial landing is marked by the promontory fort they used as a bridgehead at Baginbun, Co. Wexford. The Norman mottes mark their early advance. The castles, monasteries and towns continue the story. Later episodes in Irish history are also reflected in physical remains be they the great houses of the rich, the traces of farms and cottages of the last few hundred years or the workhouses which speak of the destitution and famines of the nineteenth century. Irish history even in periods rich in documentation, can be illustrated by a study of the ruins and relics of the past.

For the period before history the monuments and finds must serve alone. Eugene O'Curry, Professor of Irish History and Archaeology in the Catholic University of Ireland from 1854 to 1862, once said on viewing the stone circles at Lough Gur, 'What marvellous manuscripts if we could only read them'. He and his contempories laid the foundations of the study of the antiquities of the Irish countryside to enable us today to discern, however dimly, the episodes of our ancient times and see, hopefully with increasing sharpness of focus, the picture of the life of the many peoples who make up our past.

FORTS

We begin with forts not because they have any claim to chronological priority — the order in which the different types of monuments are dealt with has no such significance — but because the structures popularly known as forts are at once the most numerous and the most widely distributed of any class of ancient monument in Ireland. The word 'fort' is used as a general term because it is known throughout the country and is current in archaeological literature, even for structures that have no defensive character in a military sense. In a more specific sense we shall use the term 'ring-fort' for the ordinary forts and shall indicate that certain larger examples (hill-forts) must be regarded as a separate class.

Estimates of the number of forts of earth and stone in Ireland vary from about thirty thousand to over forty thousand. It is not possible in the absence of a complete archaeological survey to state the exact number of these structures. On the one hand some circular sites indicated on the Ordnance Survey Maps in a manner similar to the ring-forts are in fact other types of monuments; while many small ring-forts have been omitted on the maps. It must suffice, therefore, to say that the number of forts runs into tens of thousands and that examples of them may be found in almost every part of the country, though they are sparse or completely absent in the more inhospitable mountain areas.

In its simplest form the ring-fort may be described as a space most frequently circular, surrounded by a bank and fosse (3) or simply by a rampart of stone. The bank is generally built by piling up inside the fosse the material obtained by digging the latter. In stony districts there is usually a stone-built wall instead of an enclosing bank and there is normally no fosse in such cases (5,9). The fosse may be dug in rock and the broken rock so obtained piled up to form a bank, as in the manner of the earthen banks, and be given a regular stone-built facing on both sides with rock debris forming the core of the wall.

When such a wall has collapsed and when vegetation has grown over it, it is frequently, until excavated, quite indistinguishable from an earthen structure. The material does, however, provide a basis for segregating forts into two broad classes — earthen and stone-built — which classification is reflected in the popular nomenclature, but, as we shall see presently, this classification by material includes numerous variants in the matter of size, nature, and complexity of defences, shape, subsidiary structures, and other features.

Forts are referred to under various Irish terms, and these, or Anglicized versions of them, we frequently find incorporated in place names: *lios, ráth, cathair, caiseal, dún*. Of these *lios* and *ráth* are usually applied to earthen forts while *cathair* and *caiseal* are used for stone-built examples. *Dún* is less general and tends to occur in placenames to designate large forts and especially the promontory forts with which we shall deal below. The words *ráth* and *lios* (Anglicized 'rath' and 'liss') are now employed in parts of the country as interchangeable terms to signify an earthen ring-fort. A study of the distribution of these words as elements in placenames shows *ráth* to occur almost exclusively over part of the eastern portion of Ireland where *lios* is more usual elsewhere. The evidence provided by early texts, however, reveals a distinction now lost and shows that *ráth* signified the enclosing bank while *lios* meant the open space within. In places where the use of the Irish words has been abandoned these structures are most frequently referred to as 'fort', though the word 'mote' is used in some areas — particularly in County Limerick. It must, however, be noted that the popular use of this word is rather indiscriminate and we find that 'mote' is applied to various types of earthen structures.

Ring-forts vary very considerably in size. The diameter of the enclosed space may be only 15 m or 20 m or may be as much as 60 m. In the more elaborately defended examples the defences take up a much greater area than that of the enclosure. A triple-ramparted fort may have an external diameter of about 120 m, while the inner space is only 45 m in diameter. Examples larger than this are uncommon, though we find, as a distinct class, enclosures usually of much greater size which are termed hill-forts and which will be dealt with below.

Excavation has given considerable information as to the purpose of ring-forts, though ancient alterations and repairs combined with later damage by agricultural operations blur the picture. These considerations, together with the fact that in few cases has a sufficient proportion of the interior been examined, make it difficult to discover the exact arrangements within. It is clear, however, that the large majority of ring-forts had no real military significance but were rather protected farmsteads. Some measure of defence for the occupying family was provided by the ramparts and fosses within which cattle might be brought for safety from wolves or cattle raiders. There is evidence also on several sites for crafts, metal and glassworking, e.g. Garranes, Co. Cork, and slag and crucibles are fairly common finds. Such manufactures are to be thought of more as a degree of self-sufficiency of the homesteads rather than evidence for centralized trading.

In several sites such as the second ring-fort at Garryduff, Co. Cork; Tullyallen, Co. Armagh; Lisduggan and Coolowen, Co. Cork, little sign of habitation activity was found. It has been suggested that such sites were enclosures for cattle rather than farmsteads. Once again the extent of destruction and sometimes the inadequacy of the area examined leave such conclusions difficult to substantiate. It was noted at some ring-forts which furnished considerable evidence for occupation, e.g. Garranes and Ballycatteen, Co. Cork, that the evidence for activity was concentrated largely in one segment of the enclosed area. Since there appears to be no fixed arrangement of buildings etc. within the ring-forts, a very widespread opening of the site and good preservation of the ancient surfaces would be necessary before a conclusion that it remained largely uninhabited can be reached.

The building and occupation of ring-forts extended over a very long period, at least from the Early Iron Age, throughout the whole Early Christian period, and persisted into late Medieval times. The earliest dating of earthen ring-forts so far established is the second century a.d. for the Rath of the Synods, a complex site on the Hill of Tara, Co. Meath. A comparable date has been suggested, on rather doubtful grounds, for a ring-fort at Rathnew, at Uisneach, Co. Westmeath. The ring-fort at Feerwore, Co. Galway, outside of which the famous decorated Iron Age stone known as the Turoe Stone (83) once stood, has been assigned to the same period. The large majority of excavated earthen ring-forts belong to Early Christian times. Garranes and Ballycatteen, Co. Cork, have been dated to the fifth and sixth centuries respectively. Togherstown, Co. Westmeath, probably belongs to the sixth century while Letterkeen, Co. Mayo and Garryduff, Co. Cork, have been assigned to the seventh and eighth centuries a.d. Lissue, Co. Antrim, was dated to the tenth and eleventh centuries and Béal Boru in the townland of Ballyvally, Co. Clare, was occupied first in the eleventh century and strengthened in Anglo-Norman times. Medieval pottery (fourteenth century) was found in the fosses of Corliss Fort, Co. Armagh, and pottery of fifteenth to seventeenth century date was found in Ballycatteen fort though this was probably not due to actual occupation. Two earthen ring-forts at Shannon Airport, Co. Clare, one, 'Thady's Fort', in Ballycally townland and the other in the townland of Garrynamona, were dated to the seventeenth century indicating a continuance of the use and even the building of such structures to a very late period. Chance finds reported as having been discovered in unexcavated forts date from all periods from Bronze Age to Medieval times, but in many cases it is not clear if these finds were really associated with the forts.

The dating of stone ring-forts conforms with that of the earthen type though rather fewer have been excavated. Two sites, recently excavated at Aughinish Island, Co. Limerick, can be dated to the overlap between Late Bronze Age and Early Iron Age times. The stone forts at Carraig Aille, Co. Limerick, were dated to the eighth to eleventh centuries but some of the finds seem to indicate a much earlier date for the beginning of the habitation. It has been suggested that the stone ring-fort at Leacanabuaile, Co. Kerry, may belong rather to Late Medieval times than to the Early Christian period.

The number of excavations of ring-forts has greatly increased over the years and these have confirmed that the great majority of examples belong to the Early Christian period. The finds are often sparse and many such as ring-pins, combs etc., are not as yet closely dateable. In the north-east of the country, a pottery type known as souterrain ware has been found on many sites. This pottery is known not only from ring-forts but also from other sites of the early Christian period such as crannógs (e.g. Lough Faughan, Co. Down) and monastic sites (e.g. Nendrum, Co. Down). While in the north-east ring-fort after ring-fort, e.g. Lissue and Poleglass, Co. Antrim and Ballyfounder, Crossnacreevy and two at Ballywillwill all in Co. Down, have yielded souterrain ware, it remains absent in excavations elsewhere. Indeed though some imported wares, mainly of the sixth to the eighth centuries, turn up occasionally, e.g. Garranes and Ballycatteen, Co. Cork, it would appear that no native pottery was manufactured in Ireland outside the north-east in Early Christian times. Examples of the late use of ring-forts have increased, e.g. Ballyfounder, Co. Down, primarily dated to the sixth and seventh centuries but containing in the upper layers a rectangular house of thirteenth-century date.

Mention the ring-forts (ráth, lios etc.) is common in the Irish Sagas and other writings and it is clear from these that they were dwelling places at least of the better-off strata of society. There are also accounts of the making of ring-forts and it is of interest that the word to dig is used specifically in connection with the making of a ráth indicating that ráth signifies the earthen fosse and bank structure. Reference to the use of ring-forts is also found in the fourteenth century. The stone ring-fort at Cahermacnaghten, Co. Clare, was inhabited by the O'Davoren family and their law school towards the end of the seventeenth century.

It is seldom possible to relate the findings of excavation directly to literary accounts even when a site can be reliably identified. Indeed, the fact that so many ring-forts show occupation over a long period makes it hazardous to use the literary evidence as a source of dating especially for the date of the construction of the ring-fort. However, in one recent example, Rathbeg, Co. Antrim, an account of the killing of a king in 650 a.d. is of interest in indicating the importance of the site at that time. Portions of the finds, though some are of much later date, could accord with a seventh-century dating.

There are as yet insufficient radiocarbon determinations to assist greatly in the dating of ring-forts. Several determinations from Raheennamadra, Co. Limerick, indicate a date around the seventh century a.d. but the site may well have had a long period of use.

Since no good evidence has been given of prototypes abroad some archaeologists are inclined to see the ring-fort as a native development. Excavations give us hints that this conclusion may be correct. At Knockadoon, Lough Gur, there are enclosures defined by two concentric circles of upright stones. These sites were formerly regarded as stone circles (ritual sites) but there is clear evidence from the excavation of some of them that they were habitation sites where the space around a house was enclosed by a wall of which only two concentric rows of low upright stones now remain. Originally the wall must have been completed by building a bank of sods between the uprights. That these sites developed in the Early Bronze Age is shown by the large amount of domestic pottery and other finds of that period which they have produced. Also dated to the Bronze Age, and probably to an early stage in it, is a site at Carrigillihy, Co. Cork (6). Here the enclosing wall was of stone of peculiar construction, the smaller stones being held in position and given stability by uprights which were set with the long axis placed radially. An oval stone-built house stood within this wall. (A rectangular house was built later — when the rampart was in collapse.) The roughly circular enclosure associated with the field system discovered at Glenulra, Co. Mayo, and dated to Neolithic times is also relevant. A rather crudely built house stood within the enclosure. All these sites, though none is a typical ring-fort, parallel to a degree the idea of the fully developed sites of later times. However, it must be stated that the idea of an enclosure around a habitation is very widespread and occurs in many places in many periods. While such sites argue for a tradition which would perhaps favour the acceptance of the ring-fort they are not sufficient to account for the flowering of the true ring-fort so evident in Iron Age and Early Christian times, nor do they account for the notable homogeneity of the culture of the ring-fort builders. It must be remembered also that despite the lack of precise analogies abroad, somewhat comparable structures are represented in the Iron Age of Iberia. Others in south-western Britain might be cited but the possibility of Irish origins for them cannot be entirely discounted. For the present then it would seem prudent to allow for a native tradition but to consider the ring-forts as representing a powerful new impetus probably in Early Iron Age or perhaps Late Bronze Age times. They can validly be associated with Celtic people who achieved a dominance in Ireland about this time.

The walls of a stone ring-fort when collapsed, as many are, can look superficially like a broad ring of heavy rubble, though it is often possible to trace the facings of the wall. In the better pre-served examples the built masonry rises to a considerable height and the construction, consisting of well-built facings revetting a thick rubble core, is clearly visible. The banks and fosses of earthen ring-forts as they appear today represent the collapse of ramparts rather than the original state. Excava-tions have shown that at some sites the earthen ramparts were revetted in stone. Thus at Garryduff, Co. Cork and Ballywill-will, Co. Down, the walls were faced both inside and outside in stone. There is evidence at other sites showing that a facing of more or less vertical timbers enclosed the core of earth to form the rampart, as at Knockea, Co. Limerick. At Béal Boru in Ballyvally townland in Co. Clare, the inner facing was one of stone while the outer was of wood. Sods could also be employed as revetments perhaps augmented by wooden supports as at Raheennamadra, Co. Limerick. Trenches for timber palisades around the inside of the inner bank at Ballycatteen, Co. Cork, or at the inner edge of the outer bank at Letterkeen, Co. Mayo, may also be revetments. A comparable palisade or revetment trench with stone packing for the timbers was found at Drumree, Co. Fermanagh. At Letterkeen the inner bank was revetted on the inside by stonework. Some evidence for the revetment of the inner face of the ditch was noted at one of the ring-forts at Shane's Castle townland, Co. Antrim.

Several other sites show evidence for palisades or revetments, e.g. Lissue, Co. Antrim, but since a considerable number were only very partially examined no full picture of the variants in wall structure can be given as yet. It seems clear, however, that the idea of an earth or rubble core with a facing of stone, sods or timber is a common theme throughout the whole ring-fort series, both stone and earth. The presence of the ditch in those where earth is the main material for the wall would be to a large extent explained as a convenient source of material, while at the same time adding to the protection. While it may well be that the earthen ring-fort and the stone ring-fort reflect differences in building traditions the features common to both unite the whole series. A close analogy for the difference in design where stone and earth is used is to be found in the long-barrow (Neolithic burial mounds) of England where in stony districts the edges of cairns are faced with dry walling, whereas on the chalk, timber and sod facing are used with great flanking ditches providing the material for the core of the mound. As in the case of ring-forts occasional use of stone revetment even on the chalk are known.

A word must be said about the recognition of wooden structures. By careful use of excavation techniques the archaeologist can discover evidence even though the wood itself has completely decayed. This is usually done by finding the post-holes of the posts which supported the wooden structure. While nothing of the posts themselves remains (unless in exceptionally favourable — usually wet — conditions) the holes are revealed as pockets filled with a soil which is different from the clay in which they were dug. The fill is usually darker because it contains more humus than the surrounding clay when the lower ends of the posts have decayed in the holes; but if the posts were removed in ancient times the fill may not be different in colour but only less compacted, in which case the post-holes are found by feeling for the softer areas. Even quite small stake-holes can be found in this way. On some sites the plan is not revealed by post-holes but by the dark bands which mark the position of walls or the burnt clay surface which is all that remains of a wood and wattle structure destroyed by fire.

The entrance to a stone ring-fort may consist simply of a neatly-built gap in the ramparts with perhaps (as at the two forts at Carraig Aille, Lough Gur, Co. Limerick) recesses in the wall ends at either side into which fitted the two halves of the wooden gate. More ambitious are the entrances to those high, ramparted stone forts such as Staigue, Co. Kerry (11) where the gateway is an aperture in the wall, lintelled with large slabs, these carrying the upper portion of the wall at this point (8,15). Of course, entrances of this type were probably more numerous than is shown by the extant remains; a collapsed wall will not indicate the upper structure of the entrance. In earthen ring-forts the fosse is interrupted leaving a causeway opposite the entrance through the bank. The sides of the entrance were sometimes stone-built — at Cahervaglier, near Coppeen, Co. Cork, a gateway formed of upright stone slabs supporting horizontal ones was set in a stone-faced earthen rampart. At Ballywillwill, Co. Down, the sides of the entrance were found to be revetted in dry-stone walling and there were post-holes for heavy wooden gate jambs. At Garranes, Co. Cork, an elaborate series of gates, three (or possibly four) in all, defended the entrance which was a long, comparatively narrow passage between the ends of the banks and fosses. Similarly, multiple gates were used at Ballycatteen, Co. Cork. At both these forts and at Letterkeen, Co. Mayo, the sides of the entrance passage were bordered by a wooden palisade. At Letterkeen, the trenches for the wooden side-walling of the entrance ran from the stone revetment lining the inside of the inner bank to join the palisade trench which ran around the fort outside the fosse.

In some cases the gateways may have been covered — the upper part of the rampart continuing across above the aperture. Some of the very heavy gateposts as at Garranes and Ballycatteen, might be interpreted as serving not only as entrance jambs but as supports for a superstructure over the gateway. A wooden tower above the gate may have existed at Garryduff, Co. Cork.

Other features exemplified by the better-preserved stone forts, such as Staigue, are the 'batter' (inward slope) of the wall faces, resulting in a narrowing of the wall as it rises, the terracing of the inside of the walls and the provision of steps to give access to these terraces or to the top of the rampart for purposes of defence (12). The rampart would originally have been provided with a breastwork to protect those standing on the top. It is hardly necessary to state that mortar is never used in the building of stone forts, but it may be remarked that the quality of their dry-stone building is of a high standard of excellence and shows the ability of the ancient builder to make the most of the type of stone available locally, be that thin slabs of shale or large blocks of limestone. Straight joints in the walls of some of the forts (Ballykinvarga, Co. Clare and Staigue) (13) indicate gaps which gave the workers access to the interior during building, the filling of these gaps being the last part of the work.

The number of ramparts with accompanying fosses (Figure 2) around an earthen fort may vary from one to three, or rarely (as at Dunglady, Co. Derry and Carrowhubbuck North, Co. Sligo) to more than three. It must be realized that these defences as they exist today are much less imposing than they were in their original state. In the course of time the height of the bank has been considerably reduced by slip and the material from it has fallen into, and to a large extent filled up, the fosse. Excavation shows that the original bottom of a fosse may be covered by 1 m to 2 m of spill — possibly by an even greater amount in some larger forts. In many instances it has been found that the fosses were cut in solid rock, involving in the construction of the larger forts a considerable amount of labour and demonstrating the high degree of social organiza- tion which made such concentrated effort possible. Usually in forts with multiple defences the fosses and banks were con- structed contiguously — there being no space between them. In some forts, generally those with two banks and fosses, a level space intervenes between the outer bank and the inner fosse. This may be referred to as a berm — a term borrowed from military defensive works — intended as a platform on which the defenders of the outer bank could stand. We find it at the fort at Lisnashandrum East, Co. Cork, and it is a frequent feature of the forts on the summits of small hills in the Cavan- Monaghan drumlin country. In these, the bank outside the

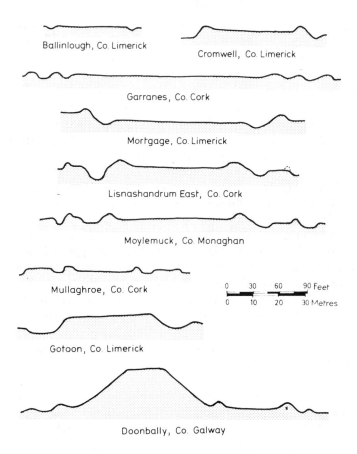

Ballinlough, Co. Limerick

Cromwell, Co. Limerick

Garranes, Co. Cork

Mortgage, Co. Limerick

Lisnashandrum East, Co. Cork

Moylemuck, Co. Monaghan

Mullaghroe, Co. Cork

0   30   60   90 Feet
0   10   20   30 Metres

Gotoon, Co. Limerick

Doonbally, Co. Galway

Figure 2   Profiles of earthworks

berm is much lower than the inner bank and sometimes has no outer fosse.

Provision for defence in ring-forts is a matter of degree. There are at the one extreme the well-defended sites with high banks, deep fosses or (if of stone) well-built walls and other defensive features. At the other end of the scale are sites with one slight bank and a shallow fosse. As already indicated these latter sites had no military significance, but their defences, even when most insignificant, must have given the farmer and his family who lived in them some feeling of security. It is difficult, therefore, to say where to draw the line between the defensive and non-defensive site when all are enclosed to some degree. Similarly, with buildings of later historic times it is difficult to draw a line when one considers the functions of the strong castle, the tower house, the imitation castle, and the Georgian house. The strong castle was inhabited by the Norman lord and his family but its purpose was largely military, the Georgian house was domestic in purpose but the steel shutters and other features that were frequently incorporated gave a measure of security.

Many of the Irish ring-forts possess underground chambers known as souterrains with which we shall deal in another chapter. Chambers are also incorporated in the wide ramparts of some of the stone-built forts — as in Leacanabuaile and Staigue, Co. Kerry, and in the central citadel of the hill-fort of Grianán Ailech, Co. Donegal. In the promontory fort of Dunbeg, Co. Kerry, these chambers formed shelters for sentries and were part of an elaborate defensive system. These features, cells and long chambers in the walls are found also in the stone forts and brochs of Scotland, which are known to have been built during Early Iron Age times and were occupied during the period of Roman rule in Britain and later.

As stated, the houses enclosed by the forts were of stone or wood and they were round or rectangular in plan. Not all excavated forts gave good house plans; sometimes repairs caused a multiplicity of post-holes which could not be intelligibly interpreted, sometimes soil conditions are not suitable for the preservation of the evidence of wooden buildings. Thus at Béal Boru, Co. Clare, a large number of post-holes were discovered but only one house plan was recognizable. This was a rectangular post-built structure, measuring 4 m x 2.5 m internally with a paved entrance in one corner. The fort at Letterkeen, Co. Mayo, enclosed two round houses, one revealed by a circle of post-holes, the other by stone slabs which formed the wall footing. At Raheennamadra, Co. Limerick, a round house about 6 m to 7 m in diameter, defined by a trench for a timber wall, was placed centrally in the ring-fort while a similarly defined round house 4.6 m in

I   FORT AT ARDSOREEN, CO. SLIGO

2   RECONSTRUCTION OF NEOLITHIC HOUSE AT LOUGH GUR,
CO. LIMERICK

3 RING-FORT AT GRANGE, CO. LIMERICK

4 BURNT OUTLINE OF HUT IN GRANGE RING-FORT

5   STONE FORT AT MONEYGASHEL, CO. CAVAN

6   RECONSTRUCTION OF STONE FORT WITH OVAL HOUSE AT CARRIGILLIHY,
CO. CORK

7 STONE FORT AT LEACANABUAILE, CO. KERRY—ENTRANCE AND HOUSES
IN INTERIOR

8 ENTRANCE TO STONE FORT, DÚN AONGUSA, ARAN ISLANDS, CO.
GALWAY

9   STONE FORTS AT CARRAIG AILLE, LOUGH GUR, CO. LIMERICK

10   TARA: "TEACH CORMAIC" AND THE "FORRADH"

11 STONE FORT AT STAIGUE, CO. KERRY

12   WALL STEPS IN INTERIOR, STAIGUE

13   WALL-JOINT AND FOSSE, STAIGUE

14   DÚN AONGUSA, ARAN: STONE FORT ON CLIFF EDGE
OVER ATLANTIC—THE *chevaux de frise* APPEARS AS A
BLACK BAND

15   PROMONTORY FORT AT DUNBEG, CO. KERRY
—ENTRANCE FROM OUTSIDE

16   STONE FORT AT BALLYKINVARGA, CO. CLARE, SHOWING *chevaux de frise*

17   DUBH CATHAIR, ARAN—WALL-TERRACES AND HUTS IN INTERIOR OF
FORT

18 AERIAL PHOTOGRAPH CAHERGUILLAMORE, CO. LIMERICK, SHOWING
ANCIENT FIELDS, ROADS, FORTS AND HOUSES

19 THE DANGAN PROMONTORY FORT, ACHILLBEG, CO. MAYO

20 HILL-FORT, KNOCKAULIN, CO. KILDARE

21   ENTRANCE TO PROMONTORY FORT, CAVE HILL, CO. ANTRIM

22   FOSSE OF PROMONTORY FORT, LAMBAY, CO. DUBLIN

23 MOTTE-AND-BAILEY, TIPPERARY HILLS, CO. TIPPERARY

24 MOTTE-AND-BAILEY, RATHCREEVAGH, CO. WESTMEATH

25   MOTTE-AND-BAILEY, DROMORE, CO. DOWN

26 MOUND AT MAGH ADHAIR, CO. CLARE

27 PLATFORM-TYPE RING-FORT, BALLINGARRY DOWN, CO. LIMERICK—
DURING EXCAVATION

28 RATH MEAVE, TARA, CO. MEATH

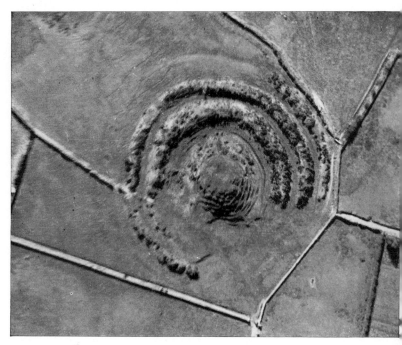

29 KILFINNANE, CO. LIMERICK

diameter was discovered at Lismurphy, Co. Derry. Within a ring-fort of Ballywee, Co. Antrim, a rectangular house plan 8 m by 16 m was defined by stones set on edge. An underground chamber discussed below in the chapter on souterrains opened from the interior of this house and a comparable chamber closely abutted the house at Raheennamadra. Conditions of excavation have hardly ever been such that the total picture at any one time can be fully demonstrated. Not only has destruction by tillage etc. often disturbed the interior so as to make the segregation of various phases within the time of use of the ring-fort very difficult but also many excavations have had to be done as rapid rescue operations permitting only very partial uncovering of the site.

The fort excavated at Leacanabuaile, near Caherciveen, Co. Kerry, though not necessarily typical because a large proportion of the interior is taken up by the buildings, enables us to form a picture of one of these sites in an approximately complete state (7). The stone walls of the houses, covered by collapsed material and debris, were found to remain to a height of over 1 m. Near the middle of the fort were a round and a rectangular house with communicating doorway, while subsidiary buildings stood against the rampart. A site in a marshy area at Grange, Co. Limerick, consisted of a low bank and fosse surrounding a single small wattle hut which had been built on a clay layer thrown up over the peat. On the clay surface the colour changes caused by the burning of the hut clearly indicated its outline (4). The Bronze Age sites mentioned below at Knockadoon, Lough Gur, and at Carrigillihy, Co. Cork, gave a similar picture of a single house surrounded by an enclosing rampart.

Excavation is not always necessary to reveal the remains of the enclosed houses. In many of the forts in stony areas the stone-built houses may be clearly traced (17). This is true of numerous stone forts in County Clare, in County Kerry, on the Aran Islands, and elsewhere. On earthen sites also the outline of an enclosed house is sometimes visible on the ground surface, especially when the conditions of vegetation are favourable. The position of the hut on the Grange site just mentioned was noted before excavation. On the fort marked on the Ordnance Survey Map as 'Teach Cormaic' at Tara, Co. Meath, the outline of a rectangular house is clearly visible. Of course, the house noted on the surface may be only the latest building on a site where excavation would reveal successive houses. On a platform-type ring-fort at Ballingarry Down, Co. Limerick (27), a rectangular house on top was found to be of Norman date but was the successor to several houses of different type at lower levels.

A word must be said of a theory based on excavations of sites on the Isle of Man. These excavations have prompted the theory that the bank of a ring-fort did not surround a free-standing house but was, in fact, the collapse of the clay piled as support against the house wall, the whole area inside the bank being roofed over. The sites investigated had a diameter of about 27 m inside the bank and concentric rings of post-holes were believed to have held the posts which supported the roof and which divided a central domestic area from outer spaces given over to workshop activities and to livestock. Because of the large diameter the pitch of the roof could not be very great, as a steep pitch would involve the use of impossibly large posts near the centre. It was, therefore, suggested that the disadvantage of the slight slope of the roof was overcome by covering it with sods. It is certain that the excavated Irish ring-forts cannot be given a similar interpretation and the literary evidence is also against it. The fort excavated at Lissue, Co. Antrim, is said to have been covered with this type of over-all roof but the evidence is not unequivocally in favour of this; a shallow trench encircling a hearth in the centre of the ring-fort may well be the base of an oval house some 12 m by 10 m. A more plausible explanation of the Isle of Man sites is that they are of crannóg type. Though not precisely lake dwellings they are sited on very marshy ground liable to flooding and the fosses were filled with water. The wavy outline of the outmost row of stakes and the concentric rings of stakes within can be paralleled in Irish crannógs and the horizontal timbers are also typical.

As noted above, in some sites houses were found placed more or less centrally; in others the houses were placed in varying positions within the enclosure. In one case (Carraig Aille,

Co. Limerick) the forts seemed to form the centre of a settlement, there being houses between them as well as those enclosed by them. At Garranes and Ballycatteen the inhabitants took advantage of the bank on the western or southwestern side as shelter from the prevailing wind, and the area of habitation was virtually confined to this portion of these forts. The evidence of occupation on the last two sites was meagre in relation to the size of the enclosures and the same is true to a greater degree of Raheenavick, Co. Galway. This fact and the strength of the banks would indicate that the larger ring-forts did serve as defensive structures — centres into which the population might be gathered in time of danger. To this extent they would have fulfilled a function analogous to that of hill forts discussed below.

Pairs of forts conjoined in the form of a figure of eight are not uncommon. More rare are groups containing greater numbers of conjoined forts; the main group at Cush, Co. Limerick, consisted of six small conjoined forts with an attached rectangular enclosure. Such enclosures have been brought to notice elsewhere, for instance in connection with the remains at Cruachain, Co. Roscommon. On the Cush site the enclosure represented the expansion of the settlement and the enclosing of a larger space in which houses were built.

While most ring-forts will be found in upland areas, they occur frequently in low-lying country. They are well represented in the more marshy districts of the Limerick plain, where they are numerous though very inconspicuous. The interior is frequently raised above the level of the surrounding area, clearly as a means of achieving a comparatively firm and dry surface. It is probable that the fosses of these structures contained water. There also occur in the County Limerick marshlands, and perhaps elsewhere, forts in which the fosse is *inside* the bank. Some of these have water-filled fosses at present and this would have been true in most cases when they were constructed. It has been suggested that these earthworks, none of which has been excavated, were intended as cattle enclosures, for which purpose the fosses would have provided a convenient water supply. This suggestion, which may be correct, runs counter to the general rule that sites with the fosse inside the bank are usually ritual in purpose. We know, however, of ritual sites with the fosse on the outside and it is not necessarily true that all those with the bank on the outside were non-utilitarian in purpose. The fosses in the majority of the upland forts would not have contained water, though it seems likely that they did, in a few cases, by accident or design. A fine example at Rathmooley, near Killenaule, Co. Tipperary, still has a considerable amount of water in the fosse, probably supplied by springs in the rock in which it was cut. A water supply for domestic purposes was not included within the enclosure of the forts — exceptions to this are very rare.

It must not be thought that all the forts are circular though this is true of the majority. Square, rectangular, D-shaped and other outlines occur. It has been suggested that the rectangular forts are later than the circular ones. This need not necessarily be true since we know that the excavation of a small rectangular earthwork, not unlike our forts in character, at South Lodge Camp, Dorset, gave evidence of Late Bronze Age dating. A large (63 m across) rectangular enclosure at North Treveneague, Cornwall, is similar to Irish forts even in possessing a souterrain, and produced Early Iron Age material.

On the other hand many of our rectangular enclosures may be the sites of 'moated houses' usually attributed to the later Middle Ages (fourteenth century onwards). On these the house stood near the water-filled moat and the bank was frequently built on the *outside*. They are common in England and occur occasionally on the eastern fringe of Wales. They are best exemplified in this country by examples in Co. Wicklow. A good specimen is to be seen at Whitechurch, near Straffan, Co. Kildare.

Mention has already been made of hill-forts — a class of antiquity distinct from the more usual ring-fort and much less common in Ireland. We have seen that many ring-forts occur on hilltops, and this is especially true of the larger examples and is a feature of their siting in some areas (as Cavan-Monaghan); but while the ring-fort may be placed on the hilltop, the hill-fort encircles the summit, its defences tending to follow the contour. The hill-fort is frequently enormous in size, enclosing as much as 8 hectares within its defences which may consist of stone-built rampart or bank and fosse. Hill-forts are common in Britain where they served as strong centres in pre-Roman times; most of those in lowland Britain were abandoned as a result of Roman policy soon after the invasion, though sites in the highlands of Wales and elsewhere were built and occupied well into the period of Roman occupation.

Recent work has raised the number of hill-forts recognized in Ireland to about fifty and excavations at seven examples have revealed many details. These excavations, while adding significantly to our knowledge, have demonstrated that interpretation from surface indications can prove to be hazardous and pending publication of full reports, any synthesis must be to a degree tentative.

Survey, however, has shown that Irish hill-forts can be broadly divided into two classes — univallate, which have one rampart, and multivallate, which have two or more widely spaced ramparts. Univallate hill-forts are the predominant type in the north and east of the country while the multivallate type are concentrated in the south and west overlapping in the Wicklow area with the univallate hill-forts. The great multivallate hill-fort of Grianán Ailech in the far north at the base of the Inishowen peninsula in Donegal is a notable exception to this pattern of distribution.

Excavations have been concentrated on univallate examples. A small hill-fort at Freestone Hill, Co. Kilkenny, consists of a rampart with external fosse enclosing an oval area of about 2 hectares around the summit of the hill which rises to about 140 m above sea-level. The fosse was cut into the rock and measured 1 m to 2 m deep and about 2 m wide. The bank was composed of rubble and earth and was faced originally with dry-stone work. Near the centre of the hill-fort an Early Bronze Age cemetery-cairn, of the type described below in the chapter on burial mounds, had been stripped by the hill-fort builders who used the stone so obtained to build a small enclosure about 33 m in diameter. The finds from the occupation deposits within this enclosure indicated a date about the fourth century a.d.

The great univallate hill-fort of Dún Ailinne in Knockaulin

townland, Co. Kildare, crowns the top of a rounded hill which rises to about 180 m above sea-level. A huge bank with a great internal fosse encircles an area of about 14 hectares around the summit. At the entrance, which lies on the eastern side, a causeway interrupts the fosse. In the central area of the fort a succession of great structures formed of concentric rings of posts — in some cases set individually in great post-holes and in others lined in palisade trenches — represent a succession of ritual enclosures. These range from about 20 m to 45 m in overall diameter. The entries to these enclosures, which represent a series of building phases, face eastwards towards the entrance of the fort. On either side of the entrance to one of them two palisade trenches run down the hill towards the main entrance through the rampart. They seem to flank an approach road across the interior of the fort. The central structures and presumably the great hill-fort itself are dated to the Iron Age, perhaps about the time of Our Lord. Other finds show some Neolithic activity on the site.

At Emain Macha or Navan Fort near Armagh, a great bank with internal fosse surrounds the top of a rounded hill. The area enclosed is about 7.5 hectares. Within the enclosure under a large mound about 45 m in diameter and 5 m high a complex series of concentric post-holes and palisade trenches indicated repeated rebuilding of large circular wooden structures, the entrance to which faced westwards towards the main entrance through the ramparts of the fort. The final phase of destruction was spectacular. While the great post structure of concentric rings was still standing a huge cairn of stones was piled among the posts and the timbers of the outer row were set on fire. A second circular area nearer the centre of the fort showed a succession of concentric trenches. These were interpreted as indicating a series of rebuildings of houses. Radiocarbon determinations suggest that these structures and those found under the mound date mainly from the fifth and fourth century b.c. and a radiocarbon date 265 ± 50 b.c. was obtained for the destruction of the great monument described above.

At Ráth na Ríogh at Tara, Co. Meath, a bank with internal fosse encloses an area about 300 m by 240 m, on the top of a low hill some 152 m above sea-level. Excavation through the rampart showed that the fosse was cut into the bedrock to a depth of over 3 m and that a strong palisade ran inside the fosse. Save for the passage-tomb of the Mound of the Hostages the interior of the hill-fort was not excavated. Immediately beside Ráth na Ríogh the site known as the Rath of the Synods, though considerably mutilated by digging at the end of the last century, proved on excavation to be a complex site with a succession of fosses and palisades showing several rebuildings of circular timber structures.

Excavations of the rampart at the univallate site on Cathedral Hill, Downpatrick, Co. Down, showed that it had been reconstructed more than once. It appears that when the earliest fosse had filled, another was dug and inside this a timber-laced earthen wall was erected.

The hill-fort at Clogher, Co. Tyrone, appeared before excavation to have a bank with internal fosse and multiple defences. However, excavation has shown that the original design was a bank with an external fosse and that the apparent multiple vallations belonged to other structures built on the site. Activity on the hill reached back to Neolithic times but a date in the Iron Age seems probable for the hill-fort. The construction of a large ring-fort within the enclosure is dated by finds of imported pottery to about the seventh century a.d.

At Lyles Hill, Co. Antrim, a bank without a fosse follows the contour of a steep-sided hill at a level of about 210 m above sea-level. Close to the summit (c. 226 m) an Early Bronze Age cairn covered a layer containing a great abundance of Neolithic pottery and flints. Sherds of Neolithic pottery were found in the bank and it is therefore argued that the enclosure itself belongs to Neolithic times. The absence of a fosse suggests comparison with the embanked, apparently ritual, enclosures (some of Neolithic or Early Bronze Age date), referred to below in the chapter on stone circles, but the rampart following the contour and the obviously strong defensive position conform rather to the design of hill-forts in Ireland and in Britain, and on these grounds a date in the Early Iron Age or perhaps Late Bronze Age is probably to be preferred.

Some univallate hill-forts have stone ramparts rather than

fosse-and-bank defences. Examples with single massive stone ramparts are the great oval enclosures at Brusselstown, Co. Wicklow and Carh Tigherna, Co. Cork, enclosing 6 hectares and 4 hectares respectively. Among the smaller examples of univallate hill-forts scarcely 1.6 hectares are Clopook, Co. Laois and Croaghan Hill, Co. Donegal.

Only one multivallate hill-fort, Rathgall, Co. Wicklow, has so far been excavated. This site consists of an outer rampart encircling an area some 7.5 hectares in extent, within which is a strong line of defence formed of two walls, set close to each other, possibly with a fosse between them. In the centre stands a stone enclosure of ring-fort type which proved on excavation to be no earlier than Medieval in date. Though the date of the main defences have not yet been determined, evidence for intensive Late Bronze Age activity was found within the area of the fort. It is likely therefore that the building of the hill-fort took place in that period or at the overlap with the Early Iron Age. As at Dún Ailinne and other sites evidence for Neolithic activity on the hilltop was discovered.

The great stone-built multivallate hill-fort at Mooghaun, Co. Clare, is one of the most remarkable of our antiquities. It has three great stone walls of which the outermost, oval in outline, measures 450 m by 300 m, enclosing an area some 18 hectares in extent. In it and on its walls stone enclosures of the ring-fort type were built — evidently with the material from the earlier structures. The famous 'Great Clare Find' of gold objects of Late Bronze Age date was discovered when the railway was being constructed in the neighbourhood in 1854 and it has been suggested that this, the greatest of our gold finds, belonged originally to Mooghaun, the greatest of our forts. There is, however, nothing to substantiate this attractive theory. Nevertheless, it recalls the finds of the great Gold Torcs reported from Tara, and the Late Bronze Age gold finds at Downpatrick and the ornamented Bronze trumpet from Loughnashade near Emain Macha.

Rathcoran is a large hill-fort encircling a mountain top (377 m) near Baltinglass, Co. Wicklow. The outermost of its two great stone ramparts encloses about 10.5 hectares. A passage-tomb crowns the summit of the hill. Around it a great stone wall built in recent years should not be mistaken for an ancient citadel. Like Rathcoran, Cashel Fort, Co. Cork, has two lines of defence. The outer rampart is of stone while the inner consists of an earthen bank with a fosse outside it.

Grianán Ailech, in Donegal, on a hill (240 m) overlooking Derry City has at its centre a massive stone ring-fort. Below this surrounding the hill are three ramparts. It has been suggested that the central ring-fort may be additional — perhaps about the sixth or seventh century a.d. — to an earlier, presumably Early Iron Age hill-fort.

Allied to the multivallate hill-forts with widely spaced ramparts are cliff-forts. At Cahercommaun, Co. Clare, a massive stone ring-fort is placed on the edge of a cliff. Two outer ramparts of comparatively light structure form great semicircles around it and run to the cliff edge on both sides. Excavations showed that the fort was occupied about 800 a.d., but some of the finds suggest a possibly much earlier date for its construction. In its design it resembles the much larger Dún Aongusa on the largest of the Aran Islands at the mouth of Galway Bay. This gigantic work stands on the edge of a sheer cliff rising 100 m above the Atlantic. The roughly semicircular citadel is surrounded by two widely spaced walls forming great sinuous loops springing from the cliff edge. Fragments of a third wall, perhaps never completed, run outside the second line. Outside this and surrounding the second wall is a broad band, 10 m to 25 m wide, studded with a mass of upright pillar-like stones set close together. This defensive device — known as a *chevaux de frise* (derived from a military term which originated when the Frisians used spikes to impede enemy cavalry) — might be considered as the ancient equivalent to tank traps and it would act as an effective obstacle to a charge by chariots, cavalry or men on foot.

A special type of defensive structure is the promontory fort, the name of which is almost self-explanatory. Economy of effort in the enclosing of a large area is achieved by building the defences across the narrow neck of a sea-girt promontory (19,22) or in some cases across a mountain spur (21). Of the inland promontory forts the most notable is the spectacular site of Caherconree on the mountains near Tralee, Co. Kerry, more than 600 m above sea-level — a triangle of land, steep-sided on two sides and defended on the third by a wall with terraces on the inner face and a bank of stones and earth. Spectacular also are the large fortresses of Knockdhu and Lurigethan where great spurs on the edge of the basalt plateau of Antrim are walled off by closely spaced multiple defences.

Probably the most astonishing of the sea-coast promontory forts is that of Dubh Cathair on the largest of the Aran Islands. Here a great curved wall across the base of a cliff-girth promontory is fronted by a *chevaux de frise* like that at Dún Aongusa. In the beginning of the last century an entrance gateway stood close to the cliff edge at one side. Before John O'Donovan's visits in 1839 a great slice of the cliff had collapsed into the sea bringing the gateway with it. A series of stone-built huts are clustered close to the wall and others along the edge of the cliffs were severely damaged by storms. John O'Donovan describes the damage wrought by the great storm on the famous 'night of the big wind' in January 1839 when huge rocks were hurled by the sea onto the clifftops. Like other cliff-edge sites some allowance must be made for erosion but any suggestion that these forts were once vastly greater in extent must be discounted.

Before discussing other Irish seacoast promontory forts it may be opportune to look briefly at the forts on Aran as a whole, since they display a notable variety and highlight the relationship between various forms of stone ring-forts, cliff-forts, promontory forts and hill-forts. We may take Dún Eoghanachta as a fine example of the stone ring-fort though like many of the Aran forts together with Staigue and Grianán Ailech, it was considerably restored in the last century. It is almost circular, about 27 m in internal diameter. The walls are over 4 m thick and are terraced inside with flights of steps leading to the terraces. The doorway now restored was little over 1 m wide. Dún Eochla has a central citadel of similar construction though it is somewhat oval in plan, about 27 m by 23 m. This is surrounded by a second rampart, at a distance of between 15 m and 27 m, which for the most part takes advantage of the ledges of the natural platform on which it was built. The fort stands on the brow of the central hill of the island and commands a wide view. It is clearly of the hill-fort class. Dún Conchubhair on Inishmaan is sited on the highest point of the Middle Island about 80 m above sea-level. It is oval in shape, some 50 m by 27 m internally, with a massively built terraced wall. An outer wall sweeps in a broad arc around three sides and links with the inner structure at the ends of the oval. The dominating position, elongated plan and outer defences clearly link this site with the hill-fort type, though the main structure resembles a great stone ring-fort in many respects. Even the great semi-oval citadel of Dún Aongusa, especially when compared with the completed ring of the central element at Cahercommaun, Co. Clare, cannot be divorced from the stone ring-fort tradition while its outer walls are equally clearly of the multivallate hill-fort type. Finally the *chevaux de frise* links not only Dún Aongusa with the great promontory fort of Dubh Cathair but also with the strong stone ring-fort of Ballykinvarga in Co. Clare, where a similar feature is found. It recurs once again in the promontory fort of Dunnamo on the Mullet peninsula, Co. Mayo, where it fronts a complex defence of walls, fosses and banks.

It seems then that the various forms of structure are closely interwoven and it appears probable that we may be dealing with varieties in function within one society rather than a series of separate introductions. The common stone ring-fort and their earthen counterparts are to be considered homesteads — the more massive of them such as Staigue or earthen examples such as Garranes providing a measure of defence even in the military sense. The elaborately defended hill-forts, cliff-forts and promontory forts imply an obviously primary function of defence.

We must now return to the promontory forts which are widely spread around the coast of Ireland. In County Mayo besides that of Dunnamo already described several promontory forts are recorded. One of these on the island of Achillbeg (19) has a rampart across the base of a promontory within which stands a ring-fort. The end of the promontory itself is divided by the sea into two smaller promontories, in each case defended by doubled ramparts. Among the promontory forts of Kerry, Dunbeg at the end of the Dingle peninsula is of unusual design. A massive stone wall, about 7 m thick, has a covered entrance with guard chambers and slots apparently for sliding timber baulks. On the inland side are a series of fosses and banks.

While it is probable that many at least of the greater promontory forts belong generally to the Early Iron Age, direct evidence for dating is meagre. Fragments of Roman pottery have been picked up at the fine promontory fort at Loughshinny, Co. Dublin, but excavation would be necessary to define their relation to the earthwork. Its position on the east coast makes it a promising site where one might hope for Roman remains to help dating. Three sites excavated in County Cork not only failed to produce dating evidence for their construction, but also showed very few signs of occupation and it would appear that they can have served only as short-period places of refuge and not as places of ordinary habitation. On one of the sites, Dooneendermotmore, the defences had been considerably modified in the seventeenth century and a dwelling built within it. Advantage was taken of the existence of many promontory forts to build castles within them. A site to which there are very early historical references is Dún Cermna on the Old Head of Kinsale and on this the de Courcys, Norman lords of the district, built a castle. Dunseverick Castle in Co. Antrim is another site with early historical associations and on it also a castle was built. The promontory fort at Baginbun, Co. Wexford, holds a special place in Irish history. It was here that the initial landings of the Normans were made and the great embankments across the headland, still sharply defined, bear witness to one of the most fateful episodes in the story of Ireland.

It has been suggested that the promontory fort on the river mouth at Annagassan, Co. Louth, is due to the historically known Norse settlement there. Even if such were found, the conclusion that the forts are the result of native activity would not be influenced. This is despite the fact that, since the times of Geraldus Cambrensis (*c*. 1147-1223 a.d.), their origins have been mistakenly believed to be Danish. Earthwork enclosures of the Viking period are known in Scandinavian countries — great works like those at Trelleborg and Aggersborg in

Denmark and at Haithabu in Schleswig-Holstein — and it is possible that the Vikings built promontory forts, perhaps as bridgeheads, in Ireland. It is likely, however, that if such exist they will be found in excavations of urban areas like Dublin, Wexford and Limerick where the Vikings established their settlements.

Several hill-forts are known from historical sources as royal seats. Tara became the seat of the high Kings of Ireland, Emain Macha was for long the seat of the Kings of Ulster, while Dún Ailinne, Ailech and Clogher were the royal seats for the kingdoms of Leinster, Ailech and Argialla respectively. Three of these great sites, Emain Macha, Tara and Dún Ailinne, have not only the internal fosse in common, a feature often taken as of ritual rather than of real defensive significance, but also the enigmatic circular post structures which can scarcely otherwise be explained. Noteworthy too is the fenced approach revealed at Dún Ailinne. In Emain Macha also the enclosures face the entry to the fort and it is by no means unlikely that the parallel banks of the so-called Banquet Hall in Tara are evidence for a ceremonial way leading to the enclosures at the Rath of the Synods. Some ancient descriptions of the inauguration rites at Tara suggest a ceremonial approach by the prospective monarch. Another royal hill-fort with internal fosse, Lisnaskea, Co. Fermanagh, was the inauguration place of the Maguires.

Among the known major royal sites of pagan times, Cruachain, the royal site of the kingdom of Connaught, stands somewhat apart in apparently lacking a hill-fort. Here, on broad ridges overlooking the plain are a large series of ring-forts and other earthworks. Chief among these is the great circular mound of Rathcruachan, some 85 m in diameter and 6 m high. It might be explained as a giant ring-fort of the platform type (see below) but the findings under the comparable mound at Emain Macha tempt one to speculate.

The occurrence of great flat-topped mounds is a noteworthy feature of royal sites and inauguration places. The site near Leighlinbridge on the Barrow which has been identified as Dinn Ríg, a residence of the Leinster kings, is a high, steep-sided, flat-topped mound. The same type exists at Bruree (the ancient brugh ríg), Co. Limerick. At Kilfinnane, Co. Limerick, is a splendid example surrounded by three concentric banks and fosses (29) and it has been suggested that it is a site named in the Book of Rights, which is a pre-Norman compilation. A somewhat similar earthwork is that at Magh Adhair, Co. Clare (26), the inauguration place of the Dál gCais. Here a flat-topped mound surrounded by a fosse, across which is a ramp, is associated with a smaller mound (probably a burial mound) and standing stones. A standing stone was present also on the mound at Bruree and the famous Lia Fáil has been often identified as that which once stood on or near the Mound of the Hostages at Tara. Tullaghoge, Co. Tyrone, the inauguration place of the O'Neills, appears to have been a triple ramparted ring-fort on a hilltop. Here once stood an ancient stone which was incorporated in a stone chair in the sixteenth century. A map and an account of the inauguration made in 1602 illustrate the inauguration ceremony. In that year the chair was broken down by Mountjoy who commanded the English forces against O'Neill.

Something must now be said about a class of defensive work which is not native in character — the Norman motte and bailey. ('Mote' and 'motte' are both used for these monuments but it seems preferable to use the French 'motte' as an indication of the fact that they are of Norman origin; we have already noted the colloquial use of 'mote' for various types of earthworks. The word 'moat' means, of course, the surrounding fosse or trench).

The motte is a high flat-topped mound surrounded by a ditch, attached to which and eccentric to it is a space — the bailey — enclosed by a bank and fosse (23, 24 and Figures 2 and 3). It has long been known that these sites were Norman, and that they held the wooden castles, built in the late twelfth and early thirteenth centuries to consolidate the invader's gains in the areas of the early conquest, before the stone castles could be erected. The Bayeux Tapestry depicts — in somewhat naïve manner — the erection of a motte and the fighting around a wooden motte-castle. Because mottes fall well into historic times and there is much documentary data regarding their erection, they have tended to escape the attention of the

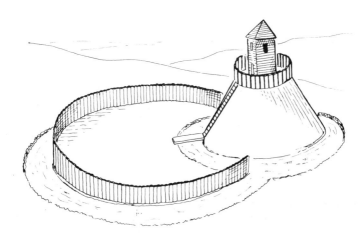

Figure 3   Reconstruction of a motte and bailey

field archaeologists, though details of their construction can only come from excavation. One was investigated some years ago at Abinger, Surrey; the top had been encircled by a palisade and the corner-posts of a square tower were found at the centre. At Doonmore, Co. Antrim, excavation showed that a rocky eminence had been occupied in the early Norman period. The rock surface had been levelled and surrounded by a palisade with retaining stone work, and a terrace at a lower level was bordered by a stone wall. The site, though not a normal motte, gives indications of the same Norman defensive technique.

The wooden tower on the motte (known as a *bretasche*, from which comes the placename Brittas) served as an observation post and as a strongly defended position for archers. The motte was usually approached from the bailey by a wooden gangway, though an earthen (or rock) ramp served in some cases or was used as a support for the gangway. In the bailey stood, presumably, the houses of the Norman lord's retainers and into it some, at least, of his cattle might be gathered for safety. It served as an outer line of defence, before retreat to the motte became necessary. The shape of the bailey usually approximates to a half-ellipse, but other outlines are known

(25); it may be subdivided by internal banks. The bailey at Knockgraffon, Co. Tipperary, is a large enclosure of irregular outline, divided into separate areas. At this site and also at the neighbouring one of Kilfeakle there are traces of ancient stone buildings. There is sometimes an inner and outer bailey, the latter less well defended than the former, as at Manaan Castle, Co. Monaghan. Excavations at the Norman motte at Clough, Co. Down, yielded finds of pottery, tools and weapons dating from about 1200 a.d. to Late Medieval times. A palisade encircled the top of the mound and associated with this were pits to accommodate archers. Within the palisade a large rectangular hall had been built and later a stone keep. No traces of a wooden tower were present but a hollow in the centre of the motte, possibly representing a cellar, could have interfered with the evidence.

The favourite siting for a motte and bailey was on a natural gravel ridge or mound — usually on an esker, but in several instances there are indications either from early historical references or from finds that the mottes were built on ancient burial mounds or on other existing earthworks. Knockgraffon is one of the sites mentioned in early historical contexts; at Rathmore, Co. Kildare, burials were found under the motte; at Knockaholet, Co. Antrim (30) and at Sessiamagaroll, Co. Tyrone, a motte was evidently built within an existing ring-fort. A very large ring-fort at Ballykilleen near Edenderry, Co. Offaly, has a motte built on the berm-like space between two ditches. On these sites the ancient enclosure served as the bailey of the Norman site. At Knockaholet the motte is placed off-centre in the fort so that space for the bailey is available mainly on one side; at Sessiamagaroll the motte is against the fort bank.

Monuments that would now be accepted as Norman mottes and also others of which there would still be question formed material of a controversy among authorities during the first decade of this century. On the one hand, all Irish structures of the motte class were claimed to be native in origin; the other side, more reasonably, claimed that certain mottes were Norman but, perhaps, did not allow sufficiently for the existence of flat-topped mounds in pre-Norman times.

Such mounds, to which we may refer as 'platform-type ring-forts', are to be found in many parts of the country. Their concentric defences and lack of a bailey distinguish them from the normal Norman earthwork, they are sometimes found in non-Norman contexts — on famous early Irish sites. We are not completely dependent on these indications as evidence of the non-Norman character of the platform-type ring-forts. One excavated at Ballingarry Down, Co. Limerick (27), gave evidence of several occupation levels and of successive additions which increased the height of the mound. While a post-Norman house had been built on the top, the important fact is that the flat-topped mound had reached its full height in pre-Norman times — probably as early as the eighth century. Within the earthwork known as Ráth na Ríogh at Tara are two ring-forts — the one enclosed by a ditch and bank, the other, conjoined to it, of platform type.

A special type of enclosure is dealt with here because of its similarity to the forts. These sites are variously referred to as *cillín*, *ceallúrach*, *callatrach* and other variants, and are marked on the Ordnance Survey Maps under one of these names or as 'Children's Burial Ground' or 'Disused Burial Ground'; the word *cill* and its variants is derived from the Latin *cella* and came to mean a church or graveyard. In general character the enclosure is frequently similar to a ring-fort, being circular — sometimes irregularly so — in outline, but local tradition tenaciously refers to it as a burial site. Until recent times such burial places continued to be used for unbaptized children, and a custom is known relating to a site in County Kerry that the first child of a family to die before reaching adult years should be interred in the neighbouring cillín. The bank surrounding a cillín is usually much less well-constructed than that around a fort and has rather the character of the ordinary field fence. Certain of these sites contain the remains of a building, evidently the early church. Excavation at Ballygarran Cill, near Waterford, gave evidence of the existence there of a long rectangular wooden building, presumed to have been a church. A cross-inscribed stone indicated the Christian associations of the place, while a considerable amount of iron slag suggested that ordinary domestic and industrial activity was carried on there. A feature, sometimes found in cillín sites, is the division of the enclosed space into two unequal parts by a dividing wall or bank. The church site may be found in the larger division, while the smaller was reserved for burial (as at Kilcolman, west of Bandon, Co. Cork), but there is no constant rule in this respect and the church is contained in the smaller portion at Duvillaun, Co. Mayo. Ogham stones have frequently been found in cillín sites — in fact these sites have been the most prolific source of ogham stones.

In the *Lives* of the Irish saints one finds instances where the local chieftain gave over his dún to the missionary who converted him to Christianity. Such occurrences would account for the ring-fort character of the cillín sites, as would also the general fashion of enclosing a site by bank and rampart. The same defensive features are found on normal monastic sites. At Inishmurray, Co. Sligo, and at Maheree Island, Co. Kerry, there are massive enclosing stone walls while Templemanaghan, Co. Kerry, is surrounded by an earthen rampart. Hilltop church sites with enclosing banks are a feature of certain areas, for instance, County Cavan, and there are examples of large hilltop enclosures with, at the centre, a smaller area which encloses the cemetery and the church or church site — as at Kilmacoo, near Kanturk, Co. Cork. The enclosing bank or wall of the cillín is generally unpretentious; the remains of buildings, when in evidence at all, are slight, while the use of the site for exceptional burial custom (of the unbaptized) is its chief distinguishing feature. The explanation of the difference between the cillín and the ordinary monastic or other early ecclesiastical site is a matter of surmise. The theory has been advanced that cillíns were originally places connected with a pre-Christian cult which were taken over in the early days of Christianity in Ireland and rededicated to the new religion but for this real evidence is lacking. Again, it has been suggested that they are the result of an early stratum of Christian activity and that there were, 'so to speak, two or more layers or strata of Early Irish Christianity'. The sites are very numerous; it has been stated that one hundred and twenty-six are known in one single diocese in which there were also nearly one hundred early churches which, after the synods of Kells and Rathbreasail, became parish churches. The cillín remains, therefore, a tantalizing subject of study on which excavation of suitable examples, where burials do not interfere with the main features, would be hoped to throw some light.

FIELDS, ROADS
AND LINEAR EARTHWORKS

Ancient field walls enclosing large areas had been noted in the
1930s at several sites in the Foyle Basin, e.g. Castledamph,
Co. Derry and Lettershanbo, Co. Donegal, on hillsides where
the peat had been cut away. In recent years excavation and
survey has demonstrated that well organized field systems
occur under the blanket bogs of western Ireland. Extensive
excavations have been carried out at Behy, Glenulra and
Belderg in north Mayo and Carrownaglogh in the same county
near the Sligo border. In the Behy-Glenulra area long stretches
of stone walls, running parallel to each other and set 150 m to
200 m apart, divide the lower slopes of the mountain into long
strips which are themselves subdivided by cross-walls. A few
smaller fields, probably tillage plots, were also uncovered and
finds from an oval enclosure and the association of the fields
with a court-tomb, indicate a Neolithic date for the fences and
enclosure. Four miles to the west at Belderg, smaller irregular
fields suggested tillage and traces not only of furrows but even
of the plough marks were found, again dating to Neolithic
times. A stone fence with wooden stakes associated with it was
of a later date because it lay, not on the basal soil as did the
others, but rested on peat which had been already well established. At Carrownaglogh a large area of ridge and furrow
cultivation was discovered. In many places in the blanket bogland of western Ireland, field fences can be seen where the bog
has been cut away. In some cases an association with megalithic tombs, noted in Mayo, seems probable. The fact that
Neolithic field fences can be recognized under bog does not, of
course, imply that such fences were not built in other areas.
However, in land free from bog, later fence building and
clearance makes it very difficult to distinguish the lines of early
fences. That such did occur is shown by a well-built wall pre-
dating an unusual passage-tomb at Millin Bay, Co. Down.

Field systems have been noted associated with ring-forts. At
Cush, Co. Limerick, adjoining the complex of ring-forts was a

rectangular enclosure which seemed to be an extension of the settlement in the forts. Earthen bank-and-fosse fences, forming irregular fields were shown by excavation to be coeval with the ring-forts. Near the stone forts (Early Christian period) at Carraig Aille, Lough Gur, were vestiges of field banks which were possibly contemporary with the forts. Certainly contemporary with the hut site of similar date — the 'Spectacles', Lough Gur (37) — were fields enclosed by stone-faced banks. Two miles north of Ballyshannon, Co. Donegal, in Twomilestone townland, irregular field banks are associated with a stone ring-fort and huts. In the neighbourhood of some early monasteries old fields can be seen — as at Ardpatrick, Co. Limerick or at Donaghmore near Maynooth, Co. Kildare. The field worker may hope to find hitherto undiscovered ancient field systems (not necessarily connected with forts or other antiquities) in many parts of the country, particularly on upland areas that have not been enclosed by modern field fences. These ancient field systems will reveal themselves as low banks and the enclosed fields will possibly prove much smaller than their modern counterparts. Of course, the question of date must remain unresolved in most cases. In many places there are abandoned fields which are not earlier than the nineteenth century when land hunger led to the tillage of mountainous parts of the country. Near these are frequently to be seen the ruins of the small houses of the farmers who lived there when the population was much larger than at present. These vestiges of fields and houses are material on which the methods of study of the archaeologist should yield results of value to the social and economic historian.

Other evidences of ancient husbandry are cultivation terraces (usually edged by large stones) on hillsides or in sloping valleys. Such terraces are found in the valley under Knockfennell Hill north of Lough Gur, but their date is not known. Small-scale terracing occurs there also on Knockadoon and is connected with the neighbouring Neolithic and Bronze Age habitations. Large long fields bounded by low banks which appear clearly in certain lighting conditions only, run over Knockfennell. A feature of some old stone-built walls is the incorporation in them of upright stones; the partial removal of the walls, leaving the upright stones in position can lead to confusion with the standing stones and stone alignments discussed in later chapters.

Ancient roads or pathways may occur in connection with early field systems as at Caherguillamore, Co. Limerick (18) (a Medieval site) or quite independently of them, and they offer an interesting subject for anyone with a love of the open country and a flair for the use of maps. Such roads he will find very incompletely recorded, if at all, and the exercise of marking them on the 6-inch Ordnance Survey Maps should prove interesting and instructive. The historian may be able to provide historical data for the identification of some of the ancient roadways, but it will usually be found that historical references are hardly detailed enough to allow of their being unambiguously connected with the archaeological findings. Remains of roads may be short stretches which have a local significance or the shorter portions may be part of greater lengths which connected ancient centres — as the Rian Bó Phádraig which is said to have connected Cashel and Ardmore. There are several other instances of names of animals being attached to roads and linear earthworks. The Race of the Black Pig on the Curragh, Co. Kildare, is not a road in the ordinary sense. Sections cut across it showed that it consisted of a trench with slight banks at the sides. It appears to have been similar to so-called 'hollow-ways' found on the English downlands; these served as cattleways linking one pasture with another.

Stretches of ancient roads and trackways, built as causeways across bogland have been discovered in many areas. Such roads, often built of logs and brushwood are known as 'toghers', an anglicized form of the Irish *tóchar*. One at Corlona, Co. Leitrim, was constructed in sections, 2 m to 3 m long, each consisting of a central plank laid lengthwise and flanked by narrower planks at each side. The planks were supported by deeply embedded stakes and the junction of the sections rested on bundles of brushwood. The track measured scarcely 1 m wide. Radiocarbon determinations indicated a date in the middle of the second millennium b.c. A closely comparable trackway was uncovered in Lullymore Bog, Co.

Kildare. Sections formed of two planks laid lengthwise were supported on transverse sleepers and pegs secured the planks in place. These narrow tracks would not be suitable for wheeled vehicles. A stretch of similar togher known as the 'Danes Road' was traced for a distance of about 1.25 km across Cloncarlin Bog, near Monastereven, Co. Kildare. Wider roadways with layers of heavy logs have also been found, e.g. at Ballyalbanagh, Co. Antrim. An example at Baltigeer, Co. Meath, was over 3 m wide. Besides the togher at Lullymore several stretches of an ancient roadway of different construction were traced. This was of gravel and marl 20-25 cm thick and 3-4.50 m wide. Occasional planks were found but there did not appear to be evidence for continuous wooden structure as was the case in the toghers described above.

Rather similar to the problem of ancient roads is that of linear earthworks which formed defensive lines straddling important routes and, to some extent at least, defensive frontiers of territorial divisions. The most famous example is the Black Pig's Dyke which is to be found intermittently between south Armagh and the neighbourhood of Bundoran, Co. Donegal. The Dyke does not form a continuous boundary and seems rather to occur in stretches straddling ancient routes often between lakes. It consists usually of a great central bank, up to 6 m high and 9 m wide, with a fosse on either side. One stretch in County Leitrim is traceable between Lough Melvin and Lough MacNean. In Cavan, near Drumgowna, portions are well preserved, the overall width of the two fosses and rampart being about 18 m. A ten-kilometre stretch in Longford, near the town of Granard, between Lough Gowna and Lough Kinale is known as the Duncla. The Dyke fades out in south Armagh but ten kilometres beyond the point where it is no longer traceable is the gigantic fortification known as the Dorsey. Here an enormous earthwork encloses a roughly oval area about 1,700 m long east-west, and 500 m wide, of about 120 hectares extent. The defences are formed of a great rampart between two fosses with an additional lower rampart outside. The overall width of the defences is about 36 m and the rampart reaches 6 m in height above the present level of the ground in the fosses which are silted to the depth of a further 2 m. Excavation has shown that the original defences included great wooden revetments or palisades. Two streams and two roadways run through the enclosure and excavation showed that a gap of some 24 m was left where one of the roads crossed through the enclosure. The great work must have been of considerable importance and it has been suggested that it formed a defence for the royal site of Emain Macha. A third great earthwork, known as the Dane's Cast, similar in many ways to the Black Pig's Dyke, runs intermittently for 24 km from near the village of Meigh in County Armagh to Searva in County Down. For the most part it runs along ground overlooking, from the east, the Down and Armagh county boundary along which flows the Newry Canal. The defences vary somewhat according to the terrain but for the most part consist of a bank on the western side flanked by a deep fosse. In places a bank is found on either side of the fosse. It has been suggested that it represents defences along the frontier of the reduced kingdom of Ulster after the fall of Emain Macha. It has also been suggested that such great linear earthworks were inspired by the Roman walls in northern Britain, with which the Irish must have been familiar. However, it is unlikely that in the conditions prevailing in Ireland in the Iron Age, such works could be considered to be defences manned in the military sense. They are, perhaps, better considered as a deterrent to cattle raiding. A similar function must have been served by the Pale, a late earthwork of much less imposing character built around the area of the same name. The Claidhe Dubh in east Cork is also unimpressive, in places hardly distinguishable from a normal field fence. It is likely that examples of such ancient boundary banks occur in many parts of the country and are by no means all known to archaeology. Their elucidation presents problems as fascinating as those of the ancient roadways.

SOUTERRAINS

Mention has already been made of souterrains in connection with forts. In many forts it is possible to surmise that a souterrain exists because subsidence indicates its position and may even show the approximate outline of the structure. In some cases the original entrance or an entrance through the collapsed roof gives access to the souterrain. More usually, however, there are no surface indications and a souterrain comes to notice only as a result of ploughing, quarrying, children digging for rabbits or such causes. Only a very small proportion of known souterrains has been found as a result of formal excavation. It will therefore be realized that it is not possible to give any accurate estimate of the number of souterrains in the country. The total must be very large — possibly almost as great as that of the forts.

The vast majority of Irish souterrains are found inside forts. Not every fort contains a souterrain, as is proven by excavations where the whole area of a fort has been investigated and no souterrain has been found. It is widely held, but difficult to prove, that not all souterrains are enclosed in or connected with forts or ecclesiastical enclosures. There are undoubtedly examples where even the closest surface observation fails to reveal traces of an enclosure around the souterrain, as at Craig Hill, Co. Antrim or Ballyglass, Co. Mayo. Furthermore, at Harryville near Ballymena, Co. Antrim, not only were surface indications of a ring-fort connected with a souterrain lacking, but deep cuttings made in the adjoining area for drains and supply service trenches yielded no evidence of a surrounding ditch. Unfortunately, however suggestive these cases may be, they are not conclusive. Again associations of souterrains with ecclesiastical sites or even with the great passage-tomb mounds at Dowth and Knowth might at first sight suggest a separation of souterrains and forts, but, as will appear below, even in these cases a connection with the ring-fort tradition may well be present. In any case, even if souterrains unconnected with forts were shown to exist the intimate association of the two types is manifestly clear.

A souterrain may be defined as an artificially built cave. It must, therefore, not be confused with natural caves such as occur commonly in limestone areas, and which were, in many cases, used as habitations at different periods. Souterrains are, however, generally marked 'cave' on the Ordnance Survey Maps.

The methods of construction of souterrains vary considerably. Some were tunnelled in the clay where this was of such consistency as to allow of its being dug into without danger of collapse. Others were similarly cut in rock, though not in the harder varieties, but in those shales and sandstones where the bedding makes it a comparatively easy task to remove the rock in flakes. These clay- or rock-cut souterrains do not incorporate any stone building in their construction, but since the use of this method of building a souterrain is strictly limited by geological factors, we find much more frequently that souterrains have stone-built walls and a roof. In these cases the method generally was to cut a trench in the clay or rock, line the cutting with stone-built walls, and roof these walls with cross slabs. Combinations of these methods are known where part of a souterrain is cut in rock or clay and part is stone-built, e.g. Kilberrihert, near Aghabullogue, Co. Cork and Toberdoney, Co. Down. Excavation has shown that some souterrains of the stone-built type did not have stone roofs but were roofed with timber. Carefully shaped recesses for the upright posts intended to support such a roof were noted at Ballycatteen fort, Co. Cork (32), while some of the souterrains at Cush, Co. Limerick, gave evidence of having been roofed in part with stone and in part with timber. The souterrain at Letterkeen, Co. Mayo, had no stone-built wall, and the roof was supported by posts ranged along the sides.

A feature of the rock- and clay-cut souterrains is the existence in them of small opes in the walls, now built up with stone, but providing, at the time of construction of the souterrain, a means of removing to the surface, through open shafts, clay or rock chips as they were cut away by the souterrain builders. Other features noted in connection with these souterrains, and less frequently in the case of stone-built examples, are trenches intended to drain off water, and chimneys connected with hearth sites marked by accumulations of charcoal. These features are well exemplified in the splendid rock-cut souterrain found at Curraghcrowley, near Ballineen, Co. Cork. Ventilation shafts have been noted in several souterrains of more normal construction, e.g. Mullagharlin, Co. Louth, and, in some cases, it has been remarked that the end of the shaft was some distance from the souterrain, placed it would appear, so as to lessen the possibility of its discovery by an enemy, and thus prevent the occupants of the souterrain from being smoked out or otherwise driven forth for lack of air.

In some souterrains there are obstructions or traps variously arranged but always directed to the purposes of making it easy for a person in the souterrain to defend himself against an unwelcome intruder. In its simplest form, this construction consists of a mound of stones or earth which, in an already inadequate passage, makes access very difficult. Sometimes a constriction or narrowing is found as at Tobergill, Co. Down, where a narrow creep, scarcely 40 cm wide and 60 cm high, joins much more spacious chambers. There are also more elaborate forms where the roof dips towards the floor and the floor steps upwards as at Aird in Co. Antrim and Craig, in the same county. To pass these obstructions a person has to wriggle uncomfortably and would meanwhile be quite defenceless against the occupant of the inner part of the souterrain. In the more labyrinthine examples of souterrains, blind passages may be incorporated to add to the difficulty of the intruder. However, it is possible that some at least of the constrictions in width and height and especially the changes in floor and roof level may have been designed to conserve warm air within the souterrains.

In plan, a souterrain may be comparatively simple or may achieve great complexity. In its simplest form, it consists of a narrow passage, sometimes of considerable length. It is more usual, however, to divide up the long passage into a series of chambers connected by tunnels barely large enough to allow a person to pass through them. These tunnels are not merely structural devices but, because of their small size, are a defensive feature in the nature of the obstructions described above. Many souterrains contain beehive-shaped chambers, e.g. Crossdrum near Oldcastle, Co. Meath, built on the corbelled principle as in the manner of the early chambered tombs (passage-tombs) and of the clochán-type huts of the western seaboard. Corbelling to a lesser extent is noted in souterrains which do not possess beehive chambers, but in which the upper courses of the stone walls project inwards to allow of their span by shorter lintels than would be necessary if the walls were vertical. Examples are known where the chambers are not all on one level but tend, as it were, to form a two-storied structure.

We have noted that most known examples of souterrains occur in connection with forts and it may be remarked that they are to be found in association with many different types of forts, those of stone and earth, ring-forts and promontory forts — but not with hill-forts. In some cases, the souterrain or souterrains are completely enclosed by the forts, in others there may be an opening outside the fort, as in the case of the promontory fort at Dunbeg, Co. Kerry (33), where the outer end of the souterrain is outside the stone rampart, and again at Cahercommaun, Co. Clare, where one souterrain led to the outer face of the rampart. Cells in the walls of some of the stone forts are constructed in a similar manner to the souterrains, and the souterrain at Leacanabuaile, Co. Kerry, led to a large chamber constructed in the wall.

An unusual use of a souterrain in a now almost obliterated fort is noted at Kiltarnaght, Co. Mayo. Here the partly unroofed souterrain has filled with water to a depth of 1 m and is resorted to as a holy well ('St Dominick's Well') at which 'rounds' are made.

Despite a popular misconception that a fort consisted of a vast series of underground chambers, in general the area occupied by a souterrain is only a small proportion of that enclosed by the fort defences. There is, however, some ground for the popular idea in those exceptional cases where very complicated souterrains occupy almost the entire interior of a fort. Such examples are known in County Kerry, e.g. at Derrymore East, near Tralee, and it has been said of County Antrim that 'whole fields are entirely honeycombed with a mass of these souterrains, forming a kind of underground village'. Recent excavations at Ballywee, Co. Antrim, have revealed several souterrains associated with a settlement site consisting of a complex of ring-forts, enclosures, houses etc. Very extensive systems such as these are, however, rare, and inadequate exploration has given rise to the popular idea that many souterrains are more extensive and complicated than is actually the case.

Besides examples connected with forts, cases of association with ecclesiastical sites are well known. In Glencolumkille, Co. Donegal, a souterrain is connected with an early church and at Killala, Co. Mayo, another lies close to the cathedral. At Caherbullog, Co. Cork, a souterrain lies beneath a church and at Killylagan, Co. Louth, though direct connection between the two sites has not been established, a souterrain lies close to a cillín. In so far as many ancient Irish ecclesiastical sites have enclosures which partake of the ring-fort tradition such associations are perhaps to be expected. At first sight the occurrence of souterrains in the great passage-tomb tumuli of Knowth and Dowth seems anomalous. However, at Knowth excavations have shown that the souterrains are associated with dwellings largely of Christian date and that the huge mound had been adapted by the cutting of a great fosse around it to form a structure comparable to a giant platform ring-fort.

Whether souterrains occur inside forts or not, it is likely that they were associated with some form of house or shelter above ground. Often this would leave no surface evidence but in excavations at Craig Hill, Co. Antrim, a roughly rectangular house of posts was discovered with a souterrain immediately adjoining it. At Whitefort, Co. Down, a souterrain trench closely adjoined a wooden house within a ring-fort. Again, at Ballywee, Co. Antrim, a souterrain ran from the interior of a rectangular stone-built house and within the fort at Knockdrum near Castlehaven, Co. Cork, a souterrain was directly connected with a stone-built hut. At Glenderry near Ballyheige, Co. Kerry, souterrains accompany huts though no evidence of a fort is present. Though some roofing of the entrance above ground would seem desirable if only to give shelter from the elements, it is possible that some souterrains were built apart from any building overground so that they would better escape detection.

Enough has been said regarding structural details of souterrains to enable us to discuss their purpose. The presence of traps or obstructions in some of them makes it clear that these must have been used as places of refuge and, in general, we must regard this as the purpose for which many souterrains were intended. They would serve for temporary security, particularly for women and children, during periods of fighting. It has been suggested that souterrains found in connection with early church sites (for instance, that at Glencolumbkille, Co. Donegal) were intended as a substitute for, and to serve the same purpose as round towers — places of temporary security where the church valuables might be stored in time of danger.

This explanation of their purpose (as refuges) does not, however, cover all the possibilities. Accumulations of charcoal, the presence of chimneys and other evidences of occupation demonstrate that certain souterrains must have been used as dwelling places, however uncomfortable, and not merely as refuges. Indeed, if the idea that the design of some souterrains would conserve warm air has any validity, they could well have provided better sleeping accommodation during inclement weather than would be available in surface houses.

Some souterrains — usually of simple construction — possess neither defensive provisions which would make them suitable as places of refuge nor hearths or other features which would indicate habitation. These examples can hardly have served any purpose other than storage — they were, in fact, primitive cellars. What commodities were stored in them is a matter of speculation — perhaps milk or milk products, such as cheese, perhaps grain. In this connection we are reminded of Caesar's statement that the Celts stored their grain in underground granaries. The souterrain at Letterkeen, Co. Mayo, was a simple passage entered at one end where there was a crude step; it had no elaboration to make it suitable as a place of refuge and must have served merely for storage. This is likely to have been true also of some of the Cush souterrains and the same conclusion has been reached regarding one at Cave Hill on the outskirts of Belfast. At Carraig Aille, Lough Gur, a deep square rock hollow associated with the house sites outside one of the forts had evidently been artificially enlarged and provided with irregular steps so as to serve for storage in lieu of a normal souterrain.

It is clear, therefore, that a single explanation as to purpose does not cover all examples of souterrains. Their structural features show that they may have been built for different reasons, and individual examples may have been used for a wide variety of purposes. It seems likely, however, that there is a unity of tradition behind the whole of the Irish souterrain building. A chronology of the different types is not known so that a sequence cannot be established either on the basis of structure or of function.

Finds from souterrains are not very numerous. However, several, e.g. Downview, West Park, near Belfast, have produced a flat-bottomed domestic ware which though not closely dateable persists through much of Early Christian times in the north-eastern part of Ireland. It is known as 'souterrain ware', but is even better represented in ring-forts, e.g. Lissue and Ballyaghagan, Co. Antrim and also in crannógs, e.g. Lough Faughan, Co. Down. Other finds of Early Christian material such as a bronze pin from under the clay and rock chips thrown up by the builders of the souterrain at Letterkeen, Co. Mayo, attest to an Early Christian date. The rotary querns at Cush, Co. Limerick, cannot be earlier than the Early Iron Age and other finds suggest an Early Christian date for the forts and souterrains there. Ogham stones (see pp.144-6) are frequently found as part of the building material of souterrains — as many as fifteen were found in one at Ballyknock, Co. Cork. This shows that these structures were built at a time not earlier than the early centuries of Christianity in this country, when ogham stones used in their construction were no longer regarded with reverence. In the Dunloe 'cave' near Killarney, ogham stones and a cross-inscribed stone were found incorporated in the structure.

The few older reported finds such as the bronze axes, one a palstave (Middle or Late Bronze Age type) and another, a socketed axe (Late Bronze Age), said to have been found in a souterrain at Aghadown, near Baltimore, Co. Cork and bronze spears from another souterrain near Holly fort, Co. Wexford, cannot, without corroborating evidence, be relied on for dating purposes. Other references in the published material mention the finds of 'urns' in souterrains, but, since the vessels in question are not illustrated, one cannot definitely say if they are really burial urns or merely domestic pottery.

The very marked association of souterrains with ring-forts strongly suggests that they are an integral part of the ring-fort tradition. On the basis of the evidence at present available we may state that the history of souterrains in this country like that of ring-forts is established by Early Iron Age times but that they continued to be constructed during the Early Christian period and may have been used, if not actually constructed, in Medieval times. Historical references are not as helpful as they might be because of the use of the ambiguous word 'cave'. Thus, when we are told that the Norsemen looted the caves of Munster we do not know definitely if natural caves or souterrains are in question. Again, the looting by the same people of the caves at Dowth and Knowth may refer to souterrains or passage-tombs. A late historical reference is found in an account of the war of 1641 when large parties of women and children were said to have been smothered or otherwise put to death in caves in County Antrim, and it may well be that refuge was taken in souterrains with which the area abounds. The numbers of people mentioned — 220 in two caves, and 63 in another — are, if accurate, an indication of the extensive size of the souterrains. It may be noted also that some ancient souterrains were used as hiding places or deposits for 'dumps' of arms during the periods of fighting in Ireland in the early decades of this century, and in fact similar structures were constructed for the same purpose.

A word must be said regarding the distribution of souterrains. They are found all over Ireland. They occur in Scotland where they are referred to as 'earth-houses' or sometimes as 'weems' (from *uamh*, a cave) or 'wags' (from *uaigh*, a grave, vault or cave). One at Jarlshof, Shetland, was found by excavation to be Early Iron Age in date, and other Scottish examples

30 MOTTE ON RING-FORT, KNOCKAHOLET, CO. ANTRIM

31 GIANT'S RING MEGALITHIC TOMB, CO. DOWN—SURROUNDING
BANK BEHIND

32   SOUTERRAIN AT BALLYCATTEEN, CO. CORK

33   SOUTERRAIN TUNNEL, DUNBEG, CO. KERRY

34   RECTANGULAR NEOLITHIC HOUSE, KNOCKADOON, LOUGH GUR, CO. LIMERICK

35   HUT ON COAD MOUNTAIN, CO. KERRY

36 STONE HOUSE AT BALLYVOURNEY, CO. CORK—AFTER EXCAVATION

37 ROUND HUT AT 'THE SPECTACLES', LOUGH GUR—DURING
EXCAVATION

38   PAIR OF CONJOINED CLOCHÁNS, DINGLE PENINSULA, CO. KERRY

39   MODERN FARM OUT-BUILDINGS ROOFED WITH STONE, DINGLE PENINSULA

40   MEDIEVAL HOUSES, CAHERGUILLAMORE, CO. LIMERICK—DURING EXCAVATION

41 *Fulacht fiadh* AT BALLYVOURNEY, CO. CORK—BEFORE EXCAVATION

42 *Fulacht fiadh* AT BALLYVOURNEY, CO. CORK—DURING EXCAVATION
(FRAMEWORK OF HUT RECONSTRUCTED)

43 BALLINDERRY 2 CRANNÓG, CO. OFFALY—DURING EXCAVATION

44 PORTAL-TOMB AT
PROLEEK, CO. LOUTH

45 WEDGE-TOMB,
PROLEEK, CO. LOUTH

46 COURT-TOMB, DEERPARK, CO. SLIGO

47 COURT-TOMB, CREEVYKEEL, CO. SLIGO—DURING EXCAVATION

48 WEDGE-TOMB, POULAPHUCA, CO. CLARE

49 WEDGE-TOMB, PARKNABINNIA, CO. CLARE

50 · PORTAL-TOMB AT BROWNE'S HILL, CO. CARLOW

51 WEDGE-TOMB, ALTAR, CO. CORK

52 CAIRN ON SEEFIN MOUNTAIN, CO. WICKLOW

53 ENTRANCE TO PASSAGE-TOMB IN SEEFIN CAIRN

54 CAIRNS S AND T, LOUGHCREW, CO. MEATH

55 CAIRN S, LOUGHCREW, CO. MEATH

56 NEWGRANGE, CO. MEATH, SHOWING SOME OF ENCIRCLING STANDING STONES

57 TUMULUS NEAR NEWGRANGE, BOYNE VALLEY

58 NEWGRANGE: DECORATED STONE AT ENTRANCE

have the stones of Roman buildings incorporated in their structural material. We find them again in Cornwall where they are known as 'fogous' and where the material found in them belongs to the Early Iron Age. Somewhat similar structures are the French *souterrain-refuges*. In Iceland, they are merely rock-cut tunnels, and not built of masonry. At least one example is found in Jutland; it is stone built and dates from Early Iron Age times. Otherwise they are not found on the Continent and nowhere are they found in such profusion as in Ireland. Their occurrence in Cornwall and in Scotland seems to be due to Irish influence. Their non-occurrence in Wales is a puzzling feature of their distribution in view of the other evidence of Irish connections there. Where and how the souterrains as a type originated is not yet clear. It has been suggested that they derive from the megalithic chambered tombs, to be dealt with later in this book, but the suggestion lacks proof. One can only say that there is a similarity between rock-cut souterrains and rock-cut tombs as also between the corbelled technique of the stone-built souterrains and that of the great passage-tombs. Souterrains present fascinating problems, in the elucidation of which the amateur archaeologist can help by planning and describing structures known to him, as our knowledge of the different types of souterrains depends on increasing the number of accurately described examples. In the examination of such structures, the field worker should, in particular, examine the roofing slabs for ogham inscriptions since many of our ogham stones have been brought to light in this manner.

HOUSE SITES

Dwellings associated with forts have already been discussed. In many parts of the country remains of dwellings quite independent of forts may be noted. These are referred to as hut sites or house sites; the latter term indicates something larger or better constructed than does the former, but there is no definite convention as to the distinctive use of the two terms. It must, of course, be understood that many ancient dwellings which were constructed solely of wood have left no surface indications and their plans can be recovered only as a result of careful excavation technique. Nor are wooden buildings the only ones that may leave no visible remains on the ground. It is instructive to study a deserted mud-walled house, built, perhaps, in the nineteenth century, and to notice how rapidly it disappears when the roof and upper portion of the walls have gone. Even stone walls may no longer be visible if the stone has been removed from all but the lower courses and if these have become covered with debris and vegetation; excavation is then necessary to reveal them. Accidental factors must always play an important part in this matter of the degree of preservation; a suitable spell of weather would allow grass to grow over the partly destroyed walls of a mud house and this would prevent further erosion, so the walls would remain visible as low banks. Again, even quite low remains of stone buildings will continue to be evident on hill slopes where the vegetation is not sufficiently vigorous to cover them and where they are not removed to allow tillage or robbed of their remaining stones.

It must not be thought that the use of wood or stone in house building has necessarily any chronological significance. In general both materials were used contemporaneously throughout the history of early building. Again, houses were frequently made partly of stone and partly of wood. To some degree building tradition played a rôle in the choice but the relative availability of the two types of material was the chief deciding factor.

Aerial photography can be of considerable assistance in revealing house or hut sites scarcely discernible on the ground. Thus at Conard, Co. Meath, the site of the famous monastic school, small enclosures may indicate huts though without excavation they cannot with certainty be assigned to the *floruit* period of the site in Early Christian times. Comparable huts have been recognized by aerial photography at Drumacoo, Co. Galway.

The earliest known examples of Irish houses were wooden structures which left no surface evidence. At Ballyglass, Co. Mayo, the wall trenches and post holes of a fine rectangular house 13 m by 6 m were discovered beneath the great central court-tomb. Radiocarbon determinations averaged 2620 ± 45 b.c. Beside another tomb in the same townland the outlines of two sub-rectangular huts were traced. At both sites the finds of flint and pottery confirm that the houses belonged to people of the same culture as the tomb builders. At Ballynagilly, Co. Tyrone, a rectangular house, from which a very early radio-carbon determination was obtained (3215 ± 50 b.c.) yielded pottery of the same type as that found in a court-tomb in the neighbourhood. At Slieve Breagh, Co. Meath, two circular post-built houses each 5 m in diameter were discovered. The finds of kite-shaped arrow-heads and polished stone axes indicate a Neolithic date. Some of the Neolithic and Bronze Age houses at Knockadoon near Lough Gur are also of wooden construction but others have wall-footings of stone. The shape varies from rectangular to round. Semicircular and rectangular lean-to structures also occur. Attention was drawn to these houses by reason of the fact that large stones of the wall-footings projected above the grass surface. Excavation showed that these were merely a foundation course which supported the wall material. The roof and the main body of the walls were supported by wooden posts, so that the stones served only to lift from the ground surface the organic material or sods used to form the walls.

Since we are principally concerned with remains that may be observed on the ground surface rather than those which are revealed by excavation we shall first look to those stone buildings of clochán type of which considerable portions or even complete structures remain. These are numerous in the west and south-west of the country — on the coastal mainland and on the islands. Clocháns are built in the corbelled method. Corbelling consists of placing courses of flat stones so that each course, as the building proceeds upwards, projects farther in than the preceding one. Thus, the sides tend to meet at the top and the roof is really a continuation of the walls, but may be completed by spanning the opening at the summit by a single large flat stone. To secure stability the walls have to be of considerable thickness in relation to their height. In their simplest form, these buildings are round in plan and are shaped like beehives. A comparable method of building is found also in certain of the chambers of passage-tombs and, as already noted, in some of the souterrains. It is a technique known in the Mediterranean area from which it may have reached Ireland at an early date. It continued to be employed almost, if not quite, down to our own day in the construction of out-offices of houses on the Dingle peninsula (39), though it will be found that the recent builders, less sure of their technique, or for added protection, have frequently completed the structure with a concrete top. Similar clochán-like buildings, presumably erected within the past few centuries, are found over some holy wells. In these, mortar was used to bond the stones, and similar combinations of corbelling and mortar may be seen, often excellent in execution, in domed portions of our Medieval castles or abbeys. Nor is Ireland the only country where the beehive houses continue into modern times. Villages built in this manner are still inhabited in the 'heel' of Italy, and certain farm out-buildings so constructed are known in Wales. Corbelled buildings, some of which are remarkably similar to Irish churches of the Gallarus type, occur in Burgundy and other districts in France. While many of these are modern, indications of early beginnings are given by finds of prehistoric and Roman date which have come from others.

A circular plan is by no means the only one used in clocháns, though this was presumably the earliest type. Others are square or rectangular or they may be round externally but square inside, as are the huts of the monks on the Great Skellig

Island, Co. Kerry. Groups of multiple clocháns are known and consist of two or more of these structures placed abutting one another (38). The corbelling technique is also used in buildings of which only the walls are believed to have been of stone, the roof having been completed with wood and thatch or other perishable material. The houses in the stone fort at Leacanabuaile were evidently completed in this way — the occurrence of post-holes inside the houses suggests that posts were used to support the roof which rested on the corbelled stone walls.

It is not known clearly how early are the first of the clocháns in Ireland. We know the principle of corbelling to be as early as the megalithic tombs, but no evidence is forthcoming to show clocháns to be as old as this. The practice of clochán-building was well established in the early centuries of Christianity in this country and most examples are found on early monastic sites, e.g. Inishmurray off the Sligo coast. Primitive churches built in a developed form of this technique — on a rectangular ground plan — are known, Gallarus, Co. Kerry, being the most famous example. It is this corbelling technique with the use of mortar added, which allows the building of more developed churches with stone roofs such as those at Friars Island, Killaloe, Co. Clare, at Kells, Co. Meath, and at Glendalough, Co. Wicklow. The stone roof of the early twelfth century of Cormac's Chapel, Cashel, Co. Tipperary and those of St Doulagh's north of Dublin and at Ardrass near Celbridge, Co. Kildare, owe something to the same tradition though the method of construction has considerably altered. A splendid example of corbelling is to be found in the lock-up cell attached to Newtownards Town Hall, Co. Down — built about 1770; large stones are used in a manner reminiscent of the passage-tombs, but mortar is employed. The corbelled roofs of the turrets in the sixteenth-century castle at Portsferry in the same County bear an even closer resemblance to passage-tomb design.

The corbel-roofed house has, in any case, a long history in Irish building. It may well begin as early as the end of pre-Christian times and continues to our own day. How much earlier it began, excavation may tell us if a fortunate excavator succeeds in finding early examples of a type of building that has changed but little through long ages. (Unfortunately, the finds from the Leacanabuaile fort with its corbelled houses, could not be closely dated; they may belong to Early Christian or Medieval times, but habitation there may have begun in the Early Iron Age.) Excavation at a remarkable Early Christian enclosure at Reask, Co. Kerry, uncovered several clocháns and a small rectangular oratory 3.50 m by 2.70 m in internal dimensions. In two instances the clocháns were conjoined like some other examples on the Dingle peninsula, Co. Kerry (38). A ring of stones just outside the walls of some of the clocháns at Reask was apparently constructed to secure a facing of turfs around them.

Surveys have shown how numerous clocháns are in some areas — as in County Kerry where the best concentration is known from the Fahan area of the Dingle peninsula. But many such huts or hut groups exist in various stages of preservation and have never been brought to notice in the archaeological literature and may not even be recorded on the Ordnance Survey Maps. Their recording and planning would repay the efforts of enthusiastic field workers.

Other house sites not of clochán type leave varying classes of surface indications. If stone has been used, it may still be in evidence on the surface, but if it is covered by the turf the outline of the house may be indicated by low banks only. Stone was used in ancient building in various ways — as uprights forming wall facings, as foundation course only or as coursed masonry. Thus in some houses of Early Christian date, round (36) or rectangular in plan, the wall was faced with large stones on both sides between which there was a filling of rubble. Such walls could not have been carried to a great height and were completed with other material or in some cases the roof may have sloped down to rest on the low wall tops. Medieval dwellings, rectangular in plan, excavated at Caherguillamore, Co. Limerick, showed this same method of wall building with double stone facings (40). An early seventeenth-century farmhouse excavated at Lough Gur, however, had coursed masonry which was certainly usual in more pretentious buildings from a much earlier date.

A group of almost fifty circular structures, defined by low

walls about a metre thick and consisting of two rings of slabs with a stone filling between, has been noted at Carrowkeel, Co. Sligo. The diameters range from 6 m to 12.50 m and it is thought that they were the protecting walls within which were erected tents or huts, but some appear to have been the walls of roofed structures. Some of the larger enclosures contain within them smaller enclosures (not placed concentrically). Because of their nearness to the Carrowkeel group of passage-tombs it is considered that they may have been the dwelling places of the builders of these tombs.

Level floor space for a hut built on a steep slope was some-times achieved by digging back into the hillside and terracing the area in front with the material so obtained. The surround of upright stones then serves the purpose of revetment as well as that of wall to the hut. An example on Coad Mountain, near Sneem, Co. Kerry, presents a fascinating possibility — it may be the dwelling place of the ancient copper miners who were active in the vicinity (35). (As well as the modern mining, there is on the mountain one old mine which subsequently became an Early Christian hermit's cell.)

When no stone was used in the construction of an ancient dwelling it may, nevertheless, leave surface indications. This has already been discussed above when dealing with the possi-bility of recognizable traces remaining from a modern mud-walled house. But, as has also been indicated, stone wall remains may become so covered over that one could not know from surface features alone if the visible banks are of clay or stone.

In marshy areas, however, where stone would have been difficult to obtain and was not used in early house construc-tion, there are remains of ancient dwellings marked by low mounds or banks, frequently surrounded by fosses. Examples of these have been excavated at Ballingoola, Co. Limerick, and while dating evidence was lacking — an Early Iron Age date is tentatively suggested — they gave good indications of the method of building a circular wooden house, presumably with wattles or other light material since there were no post-holes. Outside this a deep trench was dug and the material so obtained was piled against the house walls to give them stability and added thickness. The surrounding trench not only provided this material but provided the drainage which must have been essential in such wet surroundings. Two of the houses excavated had evidently been demolished by fire — a circumstance which was fortunate from the viewpoint of excavation as the house plan and other details could be deduced from the colour pattern on the clay surface where the burning timbers had collapsed. A third house, smaller but evidently of similar type, had not been burned and gave scant information to the excavator.

These houses conform to the construction once postulated for the Manx sites (discussed p.42), but they are much smaller — about 6 m in diameter, a modest area for roofing, as against 27 m on the Manx sites. This method of construction — clay piled against wattles or other timbers — was found also in the small hut, about 3.50 m in diameter, enclosed in the Grange ring-fort (4) in the immediate vicinity of the Ballingoola houses.

One of the Ballingoola sites before excavation had a saucer-like shape, the rim being the bank caused by the collapsed house wall. The other lacked the hollow in the middle and appeared as a low flat-topped mound, which without excavation could not be distinguished from a burial mound.

The Ballingoola sites have been dealt with at some length because they are the first of the type excavated in this country. Others not excavated are known in the same neighbourhood and comparable remains are likely to occur in other similarly marshy districts.

COASTAL DWELLING SITES

In the north-east of Ireland ancient storm beaches, now raised by as much as 9 metres above the present shoreline, are prolific sources of flint artefacts. These sites give the earliest evidence of a shore-dwelling tradition but with the exception of hearths such as that found in a midden at Rough Island in Strangford Lough, they contain scarcely any structural remains. They have usually been assigned to the Mesolithic (Middle Stone Age) times but it is now recognized that they belong at least in large measure to the period when stock raising was already practised. The huge quantity of flints found on these sites can, to a large extent, be ascribed to the debris of flint manufacturing in Neolithic times exploiting the rich flint deposits of the region.

Kitchen middens are accumulations of ancient refuse, and they are found on various parts of the coast, particularly in regions where sandhills occur. They date from Neolithic times onward. They are generally attested by a black layer containing much charcoal in which may be found potsherds, and other antiquities, as well as scattered bones, shells and miscellaneous debris. In these middens, hearths of stone are to be noted, around which the accumulation of charcoal is more marked. Sand-dunes not covered by vegetation shift rapidly as a result of wind action, and ancient middens not visible at one period may be revealed by the movement of the sand after a storm. As a result sherds, flints, and other objects are frequently not *in situ* in a layer but are found as a scatter on the surface of the sand.

The foundations of round huts — circles of boulders — have been noted on several sandhill sites, as at Whitepark Bay, Co. Antrim, and at Dunfanaghy and Doagh More, Co. Donegal. Graves have also been found on the sandhills; these sometimes consist of little more than groups of stones, but circular settings of stones or well-constructed cists (as one at Doagh More) also occur. Observations regarding finds and structures on the sandhills have resulted mainly from collectors' activities and not much systematic work has been done on these sites, so that evidence for structures other than stone settings — of houses or graves — were not likely to be noted. Excavation on the Dundrum, Co. Down, sandhills not only revealed stone-built graves but showed that one had a ring ditch around it. Post-holes and pits gave evidence of structures connected with habitation; one U-shaped group of post-holes marked the site of a hut or windbreak.

A site in the sandhills of Dooey in Co. Donegal was rich in finds. Several phases were recognized. First were a number of pits followed by the enclosure of a roughly circular area about 40 m in diameter surrounded by a fosse. The occupation of the site continued after the fosse was largely filled. Finally the site was used as a cemetery with seventy burials aligned roughly east and west. A standing stone over 2.50 m high had been erected, possibly to mark the cemetery. The stratification was disturbed not only by the shifting nature of the sand but also by the digging of the graves. The finds indicated that cattle, sheep and pigs were kept but there was evidence also for fishing, and large middens of shells showed that shellfish was an important item of diet. There was evidence as well for iron-working and bronzeworking together with craftsmanship in bronze and antler. The occupation can be assigned largely to the Early Christian period.

Though some sites like the kitchen middens of Rock-marshall, Co. Louth, do not produce evidence of domesticated animals others like Dalkey Island, Co. Dublin, have evidence for cattle at the earliest stages. Polished axes as at Sutton further indicate a Neolithic phase. It is clear also from the pottery found in some of the middens, as at Dundrum, that a number of shore dwelling sites of this type belong to the Neolithic period. It is equally clear from other finds that habitation — probably seasonal occupation — on the sandhills continued through the Bronze and Early Iron Ages and into the Early Christian period and perhaps even into Medieval times. The Ballybunion, Co. Kerry, sandhills have produced Iron Age pins and Roman coins, while bronze pins and brooches from County Donegal sites give evidence of a later dating.

A somewhat different type of shore dwelling site is the shell mound of the type well known on the shores of Cork harbour. These consist of mounds of shells, mainly oysters. Little has been found in them beyond layers and flecks of charcoal and, occasionally, stones which are said to have been used for opening the shellfish.

ANCIENT COOKING PLACES

A type of monument found in great numbers in parts of the country and scarcely noted at all elsewhere is the ancient cooking place, which occurs in low-lying marshy areas or near the banks of streams, and consists of a mound of burnt stone and finely comminuted charcoal. Such a mound is known as a *fulacht fiadh* or *fulacht fiann*. In English they are usually referred to locally under the Anglicized forms of these names — 'fulacht fees' or 'fulacht fians' or sometimes as 'deer roasts', an interpretation of *fulachta fiadh*. Tradition connects them with the Fianna, whose cooking places they are said to have been, hence the name *fulacht fiann*. They are marked on the recent editions of the Ordnance Survey Maps under the title *fulacht fian*.

The mounds of the cooking places, when undisturbed, are usually horseshoe-shaped in outline. Excavation has shown that the hollow within the mound marks the position of a hearth, beside which is a sunken trough. The floors of the hearths are often paved and the edges lined with flat stones. The sunken trough may be lined in a variety of ways. Some are lined with wooden planks, others with light, well-fitted logs. Lining with stone slabs is also found and in some cases wood and stone are used together. Sometimes the trough is simply made from a hollowed tree trunk and cases where a pit is dug in the marl without any lining are also known. All these varieties are recorded from a series of sites excavated at Ballyvourney and Killeens, Co. Cork.

The method of cooking was to light a large fire in the hearth and heat stones in it. The stones were then dropped into the water in the trough until it was brought to the boil. Similar cooking methods still continue among modern primitive peoples. After each cooking the stones in the trough would be removed and thrown in a pile surrounding the trough on three sides but leaving the side next to the hearth clear. This procedure accounts for the horseshoe- or kidney-shaped mounds of burnt stones with a considerable quantity of charcoal interspersed in them. The discarded stones have become broken and brittle from having been heated and subsequently plunged into water and such mounds can be recognized by the brittle nature of the stones, usually sandstone, in them. Not all the mounds have a horseshoe-shaped outline, and some are circular or irregular in plan. They vary in size from 3 m to over 20 m, as is the case of one near Passage West, Co. Cork, which is an irregular mound rising to a height of about two metres near the centre. In general the quantity of stone in the mound of a *fulacht fiadh* indicates the frequency with which the site was used. Sometimes a large number of cooking operations — over 200 have been estimated in some cases — is indicated and the replacement of hearths and troughs is recorded both at Killeens, Co. Cork and Ballycroghan, Co. Down. Besides the cooking by means of boiling in a pit, another method, that of roasting in a stone-lined oven, is also deduced from the findings of excavations at Ballyvourney and Drumbeg. It would appear that a fire was lit in the oven to heat the stone lining. Then the embers were cleared out and the meat was placed in the oven surrounded by stones which had been heated in the main fire. Experiments at Ballyvourney and Drombeg showed that the cooking of the meat (both roasting and boiling) could be carried out quite efficiently with heated stones. In one test the wooden trough contained one hundred gallons of water, which was brought to the boil in half an hour.

A further feature of these cooking places was the presence of huts nearby. At Ballyvourney the plan of an oval hut about 5.50 m by 4 m was defined by stake holes. This represented a wigwam-like structure of slender posts. Other huts were noted at the second Ballyvourney site and the floor of a hut with some post-holes suggest a comparable feature at Ballycroghan, Co. Down. These huts have been explained either as temporary shelters for sleeping or as meat stores. Four post-holes within the Ballyvourney hut have been interpreted as either a bed or a butcher's block. At Drombeg there was evidence for rather more permanent structures. There were two separate areas of occupation. In one a sequence was established, beginning with a shelter indicated by post-holes around a simple unlined cooking pit, followed by a hut, after which a further hut with stone-built walls and central post-hole was associated with a roasting oven. Later still on the second site, about five metres away, a stone-lined cooking trough with hearth and covered well, were enclosed in a horseshoe-shaped drystone bank. These structures, while obviously closely akin to the cooking places described above, seemed to indicate rather more permanent if still seasonal use.

The distribution of cooking places as at present known is predominantly in the southern half of Ireland. They are recorded in all the counties of Munster save County Limerick, being especially numerous in Cork where some hundreds of examples are recorded. They are also present in most of the southern counties of Leinster especially in Kilkenny where over forty specimens are known. Save for one or two examples in Sligo and Mayo and four sites excavated in County Down none are so far recorded in Connaught or Ulster. It is possible that they are more widely distributed throughout Ireland than is at present realized, and, here again, the field worker can do useful service by noting unrecorded sites. Outside Ireland they occur in parts of England and Scotland and are frequent in Wales where they have attracted little notice from archaeologists though geologists have recorded them.

Despite the very useful information obtained by excavation as to the use of these sites the finds of dateable artefacts are disappointing. Stone axes are said to have been found in some examples in County Waterford. A Late Bronze Age gold ornament (an expanded-ended dress fastener of the type known as a fibula) was found in the material of a *fulacht fiadh* near Balla, Co. Mayo; a flanged bronze axe (of the Middle Bronze Age) is reported from one near Millstreet, Co. Cork, while others in the same district produced querns. The more recent excavations in County Cork yielded a gold-plated ring from Killeens. Portions of a shale bracelet were doubtfully associated with one of the Ballycroghan sites. At Webbsborough, Co. Kilkenny, at the bottom of what was probably a wooden cooking trough, small balls of fired pipe clay were found. A saddle quern was incorporated in the structure at Drombeg.

The radiocarbon determinations range from as early as Early Bronze Age times at Killeens to fifth century a.d. at Drombeg. The evidence of the finds are consistent with a long period of currency. It would appear from this evidence and from the tradition regarding them, next to be discussed, that *fulachta fiadh* are another example of a type of monument beginning in prehistoric times but continuing into the historic period.

The cooking places are referred to by Keating in his History of Ireland *Foras Feasa ar Éirinn*. He describes them as being used by the Fianna in their hunting expeditions during the summer months (Bealtaine until Samhain) for the cooking of meats procured in the chase. In translation the passage continues:

And it was their custom to send their attendants about noon with whatever they had killed in the morning's hunt to an appointed hill, having wood and moorland in the neighbourhood, and to kindle raging fires thereon, and put into them a large number of granite stones; and to dig two pits in the yellow clay of the moorland, and put some of the meat on spits to roast before the fire; and to bind another portion of it with suagáns in dry bundles and set it to boil in the larger of the two pits and keep plying them with the stones that were in the fire, making them seethe often until they were cooked. And these fires were so large that their sites are today in Ireland burnt to blackness, and these are now called Fulacht Fian by the peasantry.

As to the Fian, when they assembled on the hill on which was the fire, each of them stripped off, and tied his shirt around his waist; and they ranged themselves round the second pit we have mentioned above, bathing their hair and washing their limbs ... and after this they took their meal; and when they had taken their meal, they proceeded to build their hunting tents and so prepared themselves for sleep.

Another reference to cooking deer by hot stones in a trough is found in the medieval tale of Mis and Dub Ruis. In passing it may be remarked that the word for the type of heating stone mentioned both in Keating and in this tale indicates granite while in the known actual examples recorded in the field sandstone is the normal type used. In *Agallamh na Seanórach*, which gives an account of the meeting of Caoilte Mac Ronáin — an old survivor of the Fianna — with St Patrick and of the tales related by the old warrior to the saint, there are frequent references to cooking places and *fian-bhotha* or hunting shelters. In these accounts reference to the use of pits for bathing is perhaps more frequent than to their use for cooking. The huts are clearly described as built of slender branches roofed with sedges. They are used for sleeping accommodation. The bedding of the Fianna is described as of three layers, tree branches, moss and rushes. The descriptions of the huts match the findings at the excavations remarkably. The accounts seem to favour the interpretation as temporary sleeping shelters rather than as meat stores.

CRANNÓGS

A crannóg is an ancient Irish lake dwelling. The name from *crann*, a tree, is due to the large amount of timber used in the construction of most of these sites. Lake dwellings are known from various parts of the world and from different times down to the present day. They differ in the manner of construction; some are pile dwellings, the houses being raised on piles driven into the lake bottom; others are built on foundations of logs, stones, or other materials on marshes or lake shores. The Irish crannóg is an artificially constructed island on which the house or houses of the crannóg-dwellers were built.

The use of island dwellings in Ireland is well attested historically and some of the sites mentioned are referred to as *crannógs* in the annals and in other historical documents. The word was introduced into archaeological literature and the crannóg as a type was brought to notice well over a century ago when Petrie and Wilde investigated the site at Lagore, near Dunshaughlin, Co. Meath, in 1839, their attention having been drawn to it by the finds of antiquities made there by men digging for bones.

The site of a crannóg presents varying appearances at the present day. It may still be an island in a lake, but in many cases it is distinguishable as a mound in a bog. Such a mound, when investigated, will be found to have been built when the local conditions were different — the surrounding area having at that time been either open water or so marshy as to make the site very difficult of access. In many cases crannógs have been revealed by the drainage or partial drainage of lakes. Many of those recorded in the archaeological literature of the last century came to notice because of the drainage programme then carried out, and others have been revealed recently by the lowering of lake and river levels. On the other hand, there are instances of low islands, possibly crannógs, which have disappeared because of the partial drainage of the lakes in which they stood. In these cases the lowering of the water level caused drying and hence the shrinkage of the material composing the island, while the growth of vegetation around it caused it to merge into the surrounding area.

The builders of a crannóg, having selected their site, made the island by laying down layers of various materials, of which peat and brushwood were the most usual, though logs, stones, straw, rushes, bracken, and animal bones were also used. Pointed timbers were driven in at the edge of the island to form a protective palisade; others placed in haphazard fashion served to consolidate the layers of material (43). Crannógs vary considerably in structure — due to different methods of building and also because of changes made during occupation, which sometimes extended over a long period. In many cases the evidence is incomplete because the sites were not fully investigated or because they had been seriously disturbed before they were investigated.

Crannógs are especially difficult sites because of water-logged conditions and comparatively few sites have been extensively excavated in modern times. In the 1930s four important examples were investigated: Lagore, Co. Meath; Ballinderry No. 1, Co. Westmeath; Ballinderry No. 2, Co. Offaly; and Knocknalappa, Co. Clare. More recently, sites at Lough Faughan, Co. Down; Rathtinaun in Lough Gara, Co. Sligo; and Loughislandreevy, Co. Down were excavated. Of these Ballinderry No. 1 gave the most complete data as to its original construction and subsequent changes. This site appears to be typical of many others where information is less complete and it is, therefore, worthwhile to summarize the details regarding its structure.

The first stage of the building at Ballinderry No. 1 (in the latter part of the tenth century) was to place in position a platform of timbers about 6 m square. Similar foundation platforms had already been noted on other crannógs and it was thought that they were made as rafts and floated over the site where the crannóg was to be built. At Ballinderry this had not been done because there was no sign that the logs had been fastened together. They were held in position by pegs driven into the lake bottom, indicating that the lake level was low when the platform was built. Around the platform and about

3 m from it, an irregular circle was marked out with light stakes. Within this small timbers were laid down, some radially and some at right angles to these. The timbers had evidently been taken from an earlier building because many of them were worked; and some gave evidence of highly developed carpentry. Over the platform and the surrounding timbers, layers of peat alternating with thin layers of brushwood were laid down; in these layers animal bones occurred frequently. Here and there the builders placed flat stones to consolidate the peat and brushwood. On this deposit timbers were placed in considerable quantity to form the foundation for a house floor, the floor itself being of carefully woven wickerwork. The timbers forming the foundation for the house floor covered a horseshoe-shaped area about 16 m across at its widest part. The open space in the centre contained the hearth; an irregular spread of ashes indicated that the fire was moved from time to time. Around the house and forming a strong fence at the edge of the island was a palisade of piles which enclosed an area 26 m in greatest diameter. The palisade varied in strength, and in general was strongest on the side where the island could be more easily approached from the land. Here as many as ten rows of piles formed the palisade. On the opposite side of the island the palisade was lighter, but scattered piles outside it appear to have been intended as an obstacle against boats. The entrance was marked by a gap in the palisade and was approached by a causeway made of a brushwood layer and protected by a row of posts on either side. The entrance and causeway gave evidence that the crannóg could be reached on foot — at least during the dry seasons. Provision was also made for boats to reach the crannóg by building a quay on the side opposite the entrance. The quay was made by laying down horizontal timbers and covering these with peat; it appears to have been a late feature of the site.

The original house on the crannóg was abandoned probably because of the sinking of its floor due to the unsatisfactory nature of the foundations. The surface was then raised by the use of material similar to that employed in the foundation layers, but with the addition now of layers of gravel. Included in the fill was a discarded dugout boat. Upon the new surface two houses were built, not centrally as in the case of the original house but near the edge of the crannóg, around the greater portion of which a new palisade was built — this time of squared planks. When the two secondary houses were abandoned a layer of white clay mixed with grasses was laid down and on this a fourth house, of which only scanty remains were recovered, was built. Finally, coins of Elizabeth and James II found in the superficial layer gave evidence of a transitory occupation at a late date.

Many of the features noted at Ballinderry No. 1 appear, on the present evidence, to be typical of the large crannógs of Early Christian times. Parallels can be found for the method of building, the materials used, the palisade and enclosed house and for the changes in structure and the late continuity of occupation. At Lagore three palisades, representing successive occupation phases, were found. Scattered piles occurred outside the palisade — as also, though less profusely, at Ballinderry No. 2 — and it is suggested that these gave added protection in the manner of the *chevaux de frise* of the stone forts. Nineteenth-century descriptions of the Lagore site indicate a system of elaborate cubicle-like structures connected with the latest palisade, which was built of planks, but the excavation did not give confirmation of these structures. The plank palisade at Lagore was, in any case, a carefully constructed feature. Slotted uprights held horizontal planks in position so as to form a continuous wooden wall around the site. At Knocknalappa a crannóg about 15 m by 10 m was formed by a layer of peat covered in stones and surrounded by a palisade. At Lough Faughan the artificial island was formed largely of layers of brushwood and peat and included some discarded worked planks and occasional wickerwork mats. The whole structure was rather less regularly laid than was the case in some other crannógs such as Ballinderry No. 1. Several hearths with clay floors, sometimes edged with stones, occurred in various places. Among the finds, which included souterrain pottery, was a wooden hub for a heavy-wheeled cart.

There is no indication that any crannóg held a large number of houses. All the evidence points to the fact that these sites were single homesteads and not villages. We may suppose that the inhabitants consisted of one family together with their servants, among whom might be included tradesmen of various classes; evidence of metal- and glassworking as well as less-specialized occupations has been found on crannógs. In the manner of its occupation the Irish crannóg differs sharply from the English lake village, such as those at Glastonbury and Meare in Somerset. The Somerset sites contained a number of houses surrounded by a palisade; they resemble the Irish crannóg because of their geographical environment but are clearly different in the social organization which gave rise to them.

Under the Early Christian site at Ballinderry No. 2 was a habitation stratum dating to a late stage in the Late Bronze Age with which was associated a wooden building and a number of small wicker structures. The wooden building was of peculiar construction. Planks with perforations to take uprights were laid on the ground in such an arrangement that they formed an approximately square house (10 m by 10 m) divided into seven long narrow bays. The house was surrounded by piles which either gave it protection or served to hold a projecting roof; two lines of piles marked the approach to the house. The wicker structures were circular in plan and of very small diameter (about 1 m to 2 m) and it was suggested that they were used as granaries. However, the similar structures with floors of cobblestones discovered more recently at Rathtinaun crannóg in Lough Gara were proven to be large fireplaces. The house was placed directly on ground level, the wicker structures were sunk in the ground, and both must have been built when the lake level was low. They represented a lake-side settlement rather than a true crannóg, but before the settlement was abandoned a portion of the surface had been raised by layers of brushwood and stones — placed over some of the wicker structures.

It is clear from the excavations at Lagore, Ballinderry No. 1, Ballinderry No. 2 and Lough Faughan, that crannógs were flourishing in the Early Christian period. The more precise dates suggested for the building of several of these sites based largely as they are on a presumed historical date for the foundation of Lagore, need revision. Historical sources show that Lagore was a royal residence in the middle of the seventh century but this does not fix the date of the first occupation either by the kings or others. It is clear that the *floruit* in the first millennium a.d. is similar to that of the ring-forts and that some examples were occupied later. For instance occupation of Lough Faughan extends to the thirteenth century, whether continuously or not is uncertain, and Loughisland-reevy, Co. Down, yielded material largely of twelfth- and even sixteenth-century date.

The lower levels of the crannóg at Rathtinaun yielded material of Late Bronze Age-Iron Age overlap with radio-carbon determinations of about 200 b.c. At Knocknalappa similar Late Bronze Age (or transition) material was found. Perhaps slightly earlier was the crannóg-like structure of Ballinderry No. 2. All three of these sites yielded bucket-shaped pottery in contrast to the general absence of native pottery from both crannógs and ring-forts in Early Christian Ireland, save for the souterrain ware in the north-east of the country. The lowering of the water level over twenty years ago exposed several crannóg sites in Lough Eskragh, Co. Tyrone, and three of these were investigated. Clay moulds, including fragments of one for a leaf-shaped sword and evidence for bronzeworking on one site, together with numerous saddle querns from it and from a second site, conform to a Late Bronze Age date. Two dugout canoes add to the evidence from other crannógs for the use of these by crannóg builders. Finds made in the last century in a crannóg in Monalty Lough, Co. Monaghan, include a bronze socketed axe and socketed dagger, again indicating the use of the crannóg in Late Bronze Age times. As frequently happens other finds from this site, e.g. ring pins, show that this crannóg was also occupied in Early Christian times.

Two islands in the North — Rough Island in Lough Enagh, Co. Derry, and Island MacHugh, Co. Tyrone — were settled in Neolithic times, but there is no definite indication in either case of artificial island construction at that early date. At Island MacHugh the Bronze Age people laid down wooden floors for their dwellings and, perhaps, placed some brush-wood at the island edge. A site which can more properly be regarded as a crannóg of early date was excavated at Rath-jordan, Co. Limerick, where an artificial island was made by laying down a stone layer over a foundation of peat, brush-wood, and timbers. The island was small, the foundation layer being about 11 m and the stone layer 8 m in diameter, and it must have been used for some short-term activity and not for lengthy occupation. A fragment of Beaker pottery found in a hearth over the crannóg shows that the date of the site cannot be later than Early Bronze Age times.

Chance finds or finds made by collectors, who in some cases ransacked crannóg sites — prolific sources of antiquities — also gave evidence of the long duration of the crannóg type of settlement. A famous example was that at Lisnacrogher, Co. Antrim; because of the splendid material it produced, includ-ing the fine ornamented scabbards of Iron Age date, it is unfortunate that it did not receive better treatment than that given it by the relic-seeking collectors. Crannógs dating from the early centuries of the Christian era are Moylarg, Co. Antrim and Ardakillin, Co. Roscommon. Occasional Bronze Age finds have also been noted from crannógs. It was usual to explain these away by suggesting that they were introduced accidentally in the structural material but, in view of the now established Bronze Age dating of some crannógs, such an explanation is not necessary in all cases. The main bulk of the museum material from Irish crannógs does, however, belong to Early Christian times and it seems clear that, however early their origin, the majority and also the largest examples are Early Christian in date.

Published lists of crannógs in Ireland enumerate something over 220 examples. The number has since been augmented by the discovery of many sites and there are presumably a great number yet awaiting discovery. Even if we make allowance for such an augmentation of the list of crannógs we must still conclude that they are not nearly so numerous as are ring-forts in this country, and their distribution is much more restricted. They are found most frequently in the area west and north-west of the central plain, but are known also outside this region, while County Antrim, well away from the main area of distribution, has a large number of crannógs. Apart from the accidents of discovery, which depend largely on the number of interested workers in the different areas (a factor which must always influence distributional studies) the concentration of crannógs in certain districts is probably due to the existence in these districts of lakes inviting to the crannóg builders.

The dating of the introduction of the practice of crannóg building into Ireland is still a matter of conjecture, but that the beginnings were early must be maintained in view of the excavated early examples which have been mentioned. The first European lake dwellings arose as a result of the fusion of the Mesolithic (Middle Stone Age) tradition of moor or lakeside settlements with the new culture of the Neolithic. In Ireland — as also in Britain (at Ehenside Tarn in Cumberland) — the Neolithic brought the same tradition of lake settlements. The Rathjordan crannóg is a true crannóg in structure, but its small size and brief period of use suggest that it grew out of special local needs — similar to those which caused the building of the stone hearths (also with Beaker pottery) in the neighbouring bog at Rockbarton. Crannóg building in the Late Bronze Age is testified by Knocknalappa and in the Early Iron Age by Lisnacrogher, and subsequently by numerous examples. It is possible that crannóg building was given a fresh impetus at more than one period — due to new incursions and to social conditions — but the large numbers of lake dwellings which we possess are the results of the continuance of an early tradition in a favourable environment in lakes and marshes.

The term 'crannóg' and our stressing of the use of timber in the building of these sites should not obscure the fact that stone was also used to a considerable extent in certain examples, for instance in many of the Co. Cavan crannógs. We have already noted the use of stone as packing, together with peat, brushwood and other materials. Stone was sometimes put in to form a breakwater on one side of the island or around the piles to keep them secure against the wash of the water. The Lough Faughan, Co. Down, crannóg was surrounded by a stone kerb and stone forms the foundation and the surround at

Bolin Island, Lough Gur. Some examples are made very largely by piling up stones and may be encircled by well-built stone walls — as the well-known example in the lake near Fair Head, Co. Antrim and those in some of the Connemara lakes. The dividing line between a true crannóg and an island fort becomes rather difficult in these cases, especially when a stone fort is erected on an island which is in part artificially constructed.

From the viewpoint of the excavator, crannógs have an especial importance not often possessed by other sites. The moisture which is usual on a crannóg tends to preserve objects which would completely decay under drier conditions. Thus, the finds from a crannóg often include articles of wood, leather and textiles, and so they give a more complete picture of the everyday life of the inhabitants than is available when all organic materials have disappeared. Apart from the objects found, the evidence from crannógs goes to demonstrate that carpentry of good quality was practised in ancient times — even at an early date. We have already noted the worked timbers of the Late Bronze Age stratum at Ballinderry No. 2 and also the foundation timbers of Ballinderry No. 1 which are, as the excavator remarks, 'good evidence for the high development of the carpenter's craft in Ireland by the Viking Age'.

The peculiar nature of the crannóg sites and their isolation from farmland directs attention to the type of economy followed by the inhabitants. It has been found that a considerable portion of the food must have been provided by domestic animals of which the bones are found in large quantities on and around the sites. Agriculture was also practised, as is shown by the querns and the agricultural implements found. It would appear that the inhabitants of the crannógs were farmers whose land was presumably on the neighbouring shores of the lakes on which their dwellings were built. Small-scale industries, such as metalworking, were also carried on as is shown by crucibles and slag found on the sites. To reach the dwellings, causeways may sometimes have been built, but in other cases boats must have been used and these boats — hollowed tree trunks — were found in some of the excavated crannógs. We have noted the existence of a boat-slip at Ballinderry No. 1; one was found also at Knocknalappa.

In general the crannógs were the equivalent of the ringforts, though built on lakes and marshes instead of on dry land. They afforded a measure of protection, and the economy of life of the inhabitants was similar to that of the ring-fort dwellers. In Ireland they did not hold village communities, as did the site at Glastonbury in England, but were similar to the ring-forts, in being homesteads of single families depending on agriculture and stock raising as the main sources of subsistence.

Structures of wood and hearths of stone are frequently found in bogs but are not necessarily connected with crannógs. A wooden hut built in two low storeys like the bunks on a ship was revealed as a result of turf cutting at Drunkelin, Inver, Co. Donegal. A stone axe found in the hut is thought to have been used in its construction. Somewhat similar huts, but of only one storey, were found at Kilnamaddoo, Co. Fermanagh. These huts may have been used for storage — butter wrapped in cowhide was found in one of them. The Drunkelin hut, built on a foundation of seasand, was surrounded by a stockade and the site is therefore sometimes described as a crannóg, but this is hardly warranted. At Cargaghoge, Co. Monaghan, a wooden house floor about 5.5 m square with central stone hearth and an approach causeway built of timbers was found under deep peat and supported on hazel and birch branches. These and other descriptions of houses and other structures in bogs are fairly frequent in the archaeological literature but the indications of date are in most cases meagre and indefinite.

Hearths due to temporary occupation of ancient marsh areas have also been found in bogs. The technique of pollen analysis (the determination of climatic sequences from the percentages of the various types of tree pollen) has corroborated the dating given by a study of the pottery (Early Bronze Age) found in some of these hearths at Rockbarton, Co. Limerick. In the case of the older discoveries (for instance, some of the houses in bogs), it is sometimes tantalizing to read that 'some pieces of very rude pottery' were found, there being no attempt to illustrate this material, which is most valuable as an indication of date. Even yet there is little doubt that structures are found in the course of turf cutting and are not brought to scientific notice, though finds of objects are much more readily reported. The remedy for this must be in the keenness of the local observer who is willing to watch for such discoveries and note them with sufficient fullness and accuracy.

MEGALITHIC TOMBS

During the third and fourth millennia b.c., there spread from the Mediterranean area, along the Atlantic coasts of Europe, northwards into Scandinavia and the north European mainland the custom of building great tombs of stone intended for what is known as 'collective burial', that is to say, each tomb contained many burials. The origin of the custom of building these tombs need not be discussed here since its discussion would lead us far afield and we would not find unanimity of opinion regarding it among archaeologists. It must suffice to say that the cult arose in the Mediterranean area and came to this country along the Atlantic route in several waves from western France, particularly from Brittany.

To these tombs is applied the name 'megalithic' (from Greek *megas*, great, and *lithos*, stone) because they are, in so many cases, constructed of large stones. As a descriptive title, however, the name does not cover all classes of megalithic tombs, since some of them are built, not of great stones, but of small slabs in the form of a dry-stone walling, while others that belong to the same cultural heritage are cut partly or entirely in rock. Some tombs of the same tradition were built of wood or sods, as in parts of the chalklands of Britain where stone was not readily available. The term 'megalithic' continues to be used for this whole family of tombs because it has long-standing currency in the archaeological literature in many European languages. It has the further advantage that, as an adjective, it lends itself to use in such contexts as 'megalithic religion', 'megalithic colonization', 'megalithic period'. 'Rude stone monuments', which was used formerly is not superior as a descriptive expression and cannot conveniently be used adjectivally. This latter objection applies also to 'chambered tombs', which has come into use in Britain; apart from this it is simple and is excellent as a descriptive term, since these structures consist essentially of a burial chamber, covered in most cases by a mound of earth or stone.

Popularly the tombs are known under various terms. The word 'cromlech', which will be found on the earlier editions of the Ordnance Maps and in the older archaeological literature, has now fallen completely into disfavour because in Brittany, from whence the word comes, it designates not a tomb but a stone circle. Its place was taken by another name of Celtic origin — 'dolmen' — but this is now usually confined to certain simpler types of chambered tombs. Names used for megalithic tombs in different districts of Ireland include 'giant's grave', 'Leaba Dhiarmuda is Gráinne', 'cloghogle'; some individual tombs have special names as Leaba Chaillighe, Leaba na Muice and so on. Terms such as 'druids' altar' or 'druids' table' have been foisted on the popular nomenclature by the speculations of earlier antiquaries and have nothing to recommend them, either as traditional or descriptive titles, since these burial places had nothing to do with druids nor were they intended either as altars or tables.

There are at least twelve hundred megalithic tombs extant in Ireland; countless others have been destroyed in the course of time, the stones of which they were built having been robbed for various purposes. In spite of much recent work — and few problems in archaeology attract such attention as do the megalithic tombs — the total number of such structures is not accurately known and some still remain unrecorded. Indeed, the classification of some sites must remain undefined because too much of the tomb structure has been removed to allow of certainty as to the complete form. It should also be remembered when we look at a megalithic tomb that we are often looking at the skeleton of the structure only, the covering mound and the subsidiary features having been removed. Thus we may see the chamber, consisting of supporting stones and roof, when the cairn of stones which once hid it has gone; or the ground plan alone may be recognizable when uprights only remain after cairn and roofing material have vanished. Incomplete tombs, or even relatively small portions of tombs, may often be ascribed with confidence to their respective types in a classification which is based on a study of more complete specimens, or on knowledge gained collectively from numbers of examples.

Irish megalithic tombs belong to three main classes — long-barrow tombs, passage-tombs and wedge-tombs — which are distinct in their architecture and in their cultural affinities. These classes represent three major colonizations by different groups of tomb builders. Variations in ground plan and other features enable us to subdivide the classes. These variations are in part introduced from abroad by the initial settlers and in part are the result of evolution within Ireland. Thus, for instance, the long-barrow class can be divided into two types — court-tombs which from the outset show considerable variety and portal-tombs which appear to be derived from them in Ireland.

Before describing the groups of Irish megalithic tombs some comment on the terminology is required. The names long-barrow tombs, court-tombs, portal-tombs, passage-tombs and wedge-tombs have recently come into use to replace more complex terminologies previously current. These terms emphasize in each case a notable characteristic of each type and form a consistent series. The word tomb is preferred to grave since it rather better suggests the overground and monumental nature of the sites. The various terms previously used will be mentioned in the description of each group and, since in most cases the initial word of the new term appears also in the older name, there should be little difficulty in co-ordinating the new terms with those previously in use.

In tombs of the long-barrow class the burial chambers are set in long, straight-sided cairns which taper from a broad front to a narrow end behind the burial chambers. The details of cairn design in the first group of Irish long-barrows — the court-tombs — are comparatively well known but much less is known about the cairns of portal-tombs. The description of the cairns which follows, therefore, depends largely on the evidence from the court-tombs but there are indications that many features of design are common to both types.

The sides and back of the cairns are demarcated by a kerb or retaining wall built of dry-stone walling sometimes with set upright stones. In many cases it is not possible, without excavation, to determine the exact outline of the cairn because collapse or interference have obscured its limits. Where set stones were used these can show the line of the kerbing even when the cairn has been severely denuded, but where dry-stone walling alone was employed collapse will usually obscure the outline even when comparatively little denudation or interference has taken place. Excavation and detailed survey have indicated that dry-stone walling was very commonly used and where set uprights were employed the interspaces were filled with dry walling which probably also gave a straight topping to the kerbs. The cairns were highest above the chambers and sloped downwards to the rear and there is some evidence that the tops of the kerbs likewise sloped downwards. Few complete cairns are available but the evidence as a whole suggests that a height of about 3 m at the highest point would be normal. Kerb heights can seldom be exactly estimated but some certainly reached a height of at least 1.50 m.

The cairns vary considerably in length. Though no Irish long-barrow reaches the great lengths of the huge long-barrows like East and West Kennet in England, each of which exceeds 100 m, let alone the colossal dimensions of Mont St Michel at Carnac in Brittany which is some 125 m long, some Irish specimens, e.g. Creevykeel, Co. Sligo (Figure 4) and Farranmacbride, Co. Donegal approach 60 m in length. Some Irish long-barrows are as little as 20 m long and a few even less but a length of about 30 m is normal as it is in the British series. The maximum width is usually about half the length.

The name court-tomb, which supersedes several terms — court-cairn, court-grave, horned cairn and gapped-partition grave — designates the group of Irish long-barrows which incorporate in their structure a ritual unroofed court (Figure 4). This court is delimited by a wall constructed of large upright stones (orthostats) or dry-stone walling. Usually the orthostats only appear but excavation has shown that the interspaces between them were originally filled with well-built, dry-stone walling so that the uprights would have looked like panels in a continuous wall. Excavation has shown that some courts were lined with dry-stone walling without orthostats, e.g. Behy, Co. Mayo. Courts may be approximately circular or oval in shape — fully enclosed save for a narrow entry as at Creevykeel, Co. Sligo and Ballyglass, Co. Mayo (Figure 4).

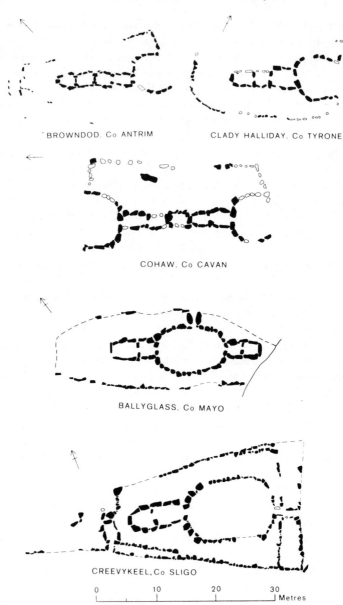

Figure 4   Plans of court-tombs
Browndod and Clady Halliday: single court-tomb; Cohaw:
dual court-tomb; Ballyglass: central court-tomb; Creevykeel:
full court-tomb.

Contrasting with this type, which are called full court-tombs, are those where the court walls leave a wide opening at the front. In this type, known as open court-tombs, the court is roughly semi-circular or horseshoe-shaped in plan, e.g. Browndod, Co. Antrim and Clady Halliday, Co. Tyrone (Figure 4). In both full and open courts a frontal facade, retaining the front of the cairn, links the court walls to the side kerbing. These frontal walls are normally more or less straight, but in some full court-tombs, e.g. Ballybeg, Co. Mayo, it is curved to form a concave frontal forecourt.

In the majority of examples a single court, which may be full or open, is set in the broader, usually more eastern, end of the cairn. Cairns with a court at both ends, each with its own burial gallery, are also known, e.g. Cohaw, Co. Cavan (Figure 4). These are called dual court-tombs. Though occasionally the cairns on this type tend to be rectangular, a trapezoidal outline is apparent in several examples, e.g. Audleystown, Co. Down, suggesting influence from the single court type where this shape is normal. A third variant which, though rare, includes some exceptionally fine tombs has a full court placed centrally in the cairn, e.g. Ballyglass, Co. Mayo (Figure 4) and Deerpark, Co. Sligo (46). The main burial chambers open from the ends of the court. The cairn in this type is widest at the centre and tapers towards both ends.

The burial gallery opens from the inner end of the court and its entry is marked by two well-matched jambstones. The gallery consists of two, three or four chambers divided from each other by jambs. Sometimes a sillstone crosses the space between the jambs. Instead of the sill which would allow access to the next chamber, higher slabs, called septal-stones, completely closing the gap between the jambs, are also frequently present. Lintels were laid across the jambs both at the entrance and at the division between the chambers but the main roofing was formed of slabs laid not directly on the sidestones but in layers of projecting stones (corbels) which slightly narrowed the space to be spanned and gave increased height to the roof. In most cases the roofing is now incomplete but some well-preserved examples are known, e.g. Carrowbeagh, Co. Mayo. The chambers of court-tombs would appear normally to have allowed adequate headroom, 2 m or so in height, but the original floor is now usually deeply covered in debris and silting which make the interiors much less roomy and impressive than they were in their original state. The cairn enveloped the chamber and filled the area between the kerbs, frontal facade and court.

Besides the main galleries extra chambers set in the sides of the cairn occur fairly frequently. Pairs of such chambers placed on opposite sides of the cairn, behind the main gallery, are present in several sites, e.g. Cregganconroe, Co. Tyrone and Annaghmare, Co. Armagh. At Creevykeel, Co. Sligo (Figure 4) besides the two well-matched lateral chambers there are traces of at least one other extra chamber while at Tullyskeherny, Co. Leitrim no less than six extra chambers are present. The entrance to the extra chambers is marked by a pair of jambs, often with a sill or septal between them. Sometimes these chambers open directly to the kerb but frequently a narrow passageway connects them to the cairn edge. In a few Donegal sites extra chambers are found opening from the courts as at Malin More ('Cloghanmore') and Farranmacbride. Extra chambers opening from the gallery itself are rare and are confined to the western part of the distribution. In some of these, e.g. Treanmore, Co. Sligo and Behy, Co. Mayo, a pair of opposing side chambers open like transepts from the main chamber. This feature compares closely with British sites like Notgrove and Nympsfield in Gloucestershire and to tombs near the mouth of the Loire in France.

The distribution of court tombs in Ireland is almost entirely confined to the northern part of the country, north of the central plain (Figure 5). In the eastern part of the court-tomb area the simpler open-court type is found, while the elaborate full court examples occur mainly in the west — Sligo, Mayo, and Donegal. Two theories have been put forward to explain the distribution pattern. One is that the builders entered the country in the neighbourhood of Carlingford Lough and that in the movement westward more elaborate tomb forms developed. The other theory postulates an entry in the west, possibly in the neighbourhood of Kilalla Bay, Co. Mayo, where there is a concentration of full court-tombs, and argues a

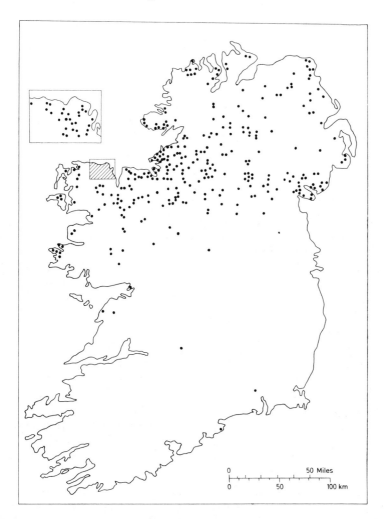

Figure 5 Distribution map of court-tombs

simplification of the tomb type in the course of an eastward expansion. The first theory was originally put forward about forty-five years ago when less than a quarter of the 330 court-tombs now known were recognized and when the great western concentrations were virtually undiscovered. The great strength of these concentrations, which include many of the finest tombs of the whole series, clearly favours the western foci as primary. The evolution of court form and chamber features and especially the occurrence of transeptal sites, closely analogous to French and British examples, also points to a beginning of the Irish sequence in the west. From Antrim and the Carlingford region a continuation of the movement to western Scotland and the Isle of Man accords with the development of the tomb features.

Excavation has produced evidence of a Neolithic date for the court-tombs. They have yielded leaf- and lozenge-shaped arrow-heads, lance-heads and hollow-scrapers of flint and chert together with round-bottomed shouldered bowls of hard smooth ware related to the 'Windmill Hill' fabrics found in Britain. A large number of open court-tombs (including dual court examples) have been investigated, mainly in eastern Ulster, and several full-court monuments in the west. The dating evidence from the full court examples is parallel to that from the simpler structures and does not as yet warrant a judgement between the theory of east-west evolution or that of west-east devolution. The finds from court-tombs present coherent evidence for a Neolithic dating and this is confirmed by radiocarbon determinations. It is clear that examples of both the simpler and the more complex types were built in Neolithic times.

There is a clear cousinly relationship between the long-barrows of southern Britain and the Irish court-tombs. Very close anologies are apparent in cairn design and orientation and the transeptal chambers and extra chambers in both series have also a great deal in common. It is likely that both the British and Irish groups derive from north-west France where prototypes for many features of cairn and chambers of both the Irish and British series can be found. It must, however, be stressed that no court of the Irish form has come to light in France, though there, as yet, the evidence for the structure of the ends of long-barrows is very scant. Further afield the 'giants' tombs' of Sardinia and the Neolithic temples of Malta suggest comparison with the Irish open and full courts but, even if these reflect some general relationship in ritual or cult, the distances involved and difficulties of chronology would make any theory of close association between the Irish and Mediterranean sites at best speculative. It is almost equally difficult to connect the Irish courts with the settings, sometimes circular, found in the front of some Iberian passage-tombs.

At any rate the court-tombs of Ireland extending into south-west Scotland, together with the long-barrows of southern and eastern Britain, can be seen as representing major colonizing movements by early farming communities covering much of the two islands. In both lands the tomb builders show a preference for light, well-drained soils, relatively free of heavy forest and suitable for primitive agriculture and stock raising. To these first long-barrow folk, more than to any other group, can be attributed the establishment of farming and the first real step towards a progressive settled economy. The great strength of the long-barrow tradition is further demonstrated by the portal-tombs which can be seen as derivations of the court-tombs.

Portal-tombs were previously called portal-graves and portal dolmens. The term 'dolmen' while sometimes used for megalithic tombs in general, has tended to be applied to those tombs of relatively simple construction with a single chamber and large single capstone. Such a description could refer to simple variants of all the three major classes of Irish megalithic tombs and the use of the term 'dolmen' can misleadingly suggest close relationships between radically different types. In a specific term it is therefore best avoided. Portal-tombs are almost always single chambered (Figure 6) though a few two-chambered examples are known as at Ballyrenan, Co. Tyrone and probably Brennanstown, Co. Dublin. A pair of tall, well-matched upright stones form impressive entry jambs. In many examples a slab set between the portal jambs closes the entry, e.g. Haroldstown, Co. Carlow (69), though in some cases a lower stone is used. The front of the capstone, which is usually the more massive end, is poised on the jambs completing the characteristically impressive entrance from which the type is named. The capstone slopes downwards from the portals and is supported also on the backstone rather than on the sidestones

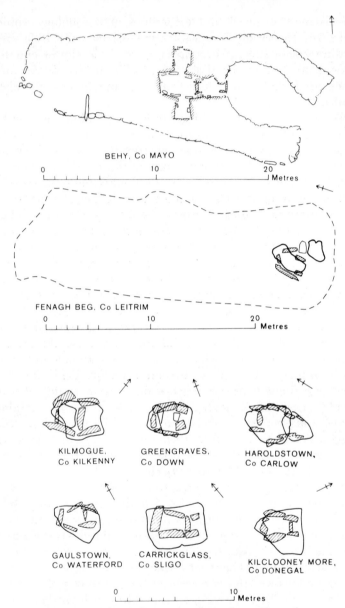

BEHY, Co MAYO

0   10   20
| | | Metres

FENAGH BEG, Co LEITRIM

0   10   20
| | | Metres

KILMOGUE,
Co KILKENNY

GREENGRAVES,
Co DOWN

HAROLDSTOWN,
Co CARLOW

GAULSTOWN,
Co WATERFORD

CARRICKGLASS,
Co SLIGO

KILCLOONEY MORE,
Co DONEGAL

0   10
| | Metres

Figure 6   Plans of court-tombs and portal-tombs
Behy: transeptal court-tomb; Fenagh Beg. portal-tomb in long
cairn; Kilmogue, Greengraves, Haroldstown, Gaulstown,
Carrickglass, Kilclooney More: portal-tomb chambers.

of the chamber. Sometimes a second smaller roofing stone is laid above the backstone with the main capstone resting upon it as at Ballynageeragh, Co. Waterford (70) and Kilmogue, Co. Kilkenny. The sidestones of the chamber, though frequently massive, are often not set in sockets but lie tilted inwards against the entry portals and backstone. Though by no means a universal rule the chamber frequently tapers from front to rear. The chambers can be of impressive height, often reaching two and sometimes three metres at the portals as at Knockeen, Co. Waterford. The floor space within the chamber, however, is usually comparatively small. Furthermore, though many portal-tombs are massively constructed, others of precisely similar design are relatively lightly built and appear diminutive by comparison, e.g. Bin, Co. Donegal and Carrickacroy, Co. Cavan.

Though the portal-tombs lack the complicated structure or elaborate building techniques of other megalithic tombs they are, especially in their denuded state, among the most spectacular of our field monuments. The method of raising such immense capstones (the largest, that at Browne's Hill, Co. Carlow (50), has been estimated at 100 tonnes) is a constant source of speculation and wonder. We know little of the actual methods used by the megalithic tomb builders and we can only guess that wooden levers and props of stone or wood and perhaps ramps overlaid by timber rails were probably employed.

The cairns of portal-tombs are often poorly preserved and many examples are completely denuded. Surveys and excavation in recent years have shown acceptable evidence for long cairns in about 25 sites of a total of some 160 Irish examples. These cairns resemble those of court-tombs though they appear to be somewhat narrower and to taper less sharply to the rear as at Ballyvennaght, Co. Antrim and at the excavated site at Ballykeel, Co. Armagh. At Ballykeel evidence for a drywalled kerb was present. Though in a few cases traces of possible round cairns have been noted no reliable example has yet been attested.

Occasionally the capstone is found poised on the portals and backstone while all the sidestones and cairn have been stripped away. Such so-called 'Tripod Dolmens' have sometimes been treated as a special class but they are merely skeletons of normal portal-tombs, e.g. Legananny, Co. Down (68) and Proleek, Co. Louth (44). There is sufficient evidence from several sites to show that the space between the sidestones and the capstone was filled by a form of corbelling as at one of the tombs at Burren, Co. Cavan. Some such device would in any case be necessary to keep the cairn which originally enveloped the chamber from collapsing into it.

Portal chambers are normally set into the end of the long-barrow. There was evidence for a shallow concave court at Ticloy, Co. Antrim, and in several cases stones flanking one or both sides of the portal indicate some form of incurved facade, e.g. Tirnoney, Co. Derry. In a number of cases more than one chamber was included under one cairn. At one of the sites at Ballyvennaght, Co. Antrim, a portal chamber stands at each end of a long cairn suggesting comparison with the arrangement in dual court-tombs. At Ballyrenan, Co. Tyrone, two portal chambers stand in line in a long cairn, while at Kilclooney, Co. Donegal, a miniature portal chamber stands close to a massive example within the same cairn. A most remarkable assemblage of portal chambers is found at Malin More, Co. Donegal. Here between two huge portal chambers placed about 90 m apart are four miniature examples more or less evenly spaced and facing at right angles to the line of the larger chambers. It is possible that the whole complex was originally covered in one very long cairn. Here, as in some other sites, e.g. Melkagh, Co. Longford, the small chambers look like subsidiaries to the large ones.

The portal-tombs in cairn form exhibit entry features and subsidiary chambers which point to the closest connections with court-tombs. This is borne out by close similarities in the finds — pottery and leaf- and lozenge-shaped arrow and javelin heads and hollow-scrapers. The distribution of Irish portal-tombs (Figure 7) overlaps considerably with that of the court-tombs. Over two-thirds lie in the court-tomb province north of the central plain. They are especially numerous in Cos Tyrone and Donegal and an origin in mid-Ulster, where court-tombs with extra chambers are well represented, seems likely.

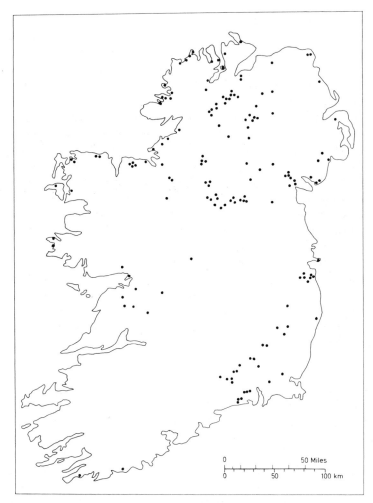

Figure 7   Distribution map of portal-tombs

However, an extension into eastern Leinster and Waterford goes outside the court-tomb region and the type is also found in western Wales and Cornwall. In general the portal-tombs do not differ from the court-tombs very greatly in the type of land they occupy but they show a marked tendency to be sited in valley positions often close to streams, e.g. Brennanstown, Co. Dublin and Ballykeel, Co. Armagh. The availability of suitable building material — especially a great glacial erratic to provide the capstone — may have influenced the siting of individual tombs. However, the occurrence of portal-tombs in more-or-less sheltered valleys may indicate a greater penetration of more heavily wooded land than that chosen by the court-tomb builders.

While the number of known Irish passage-tombs is smaller than the total of either of the two other major classes (long-barrow and wedge-tomb) there are included among them much more spectacular monuments and very important groups. Indeed certain examples of this class must be placed with the greatest known prehistoric remains — great structures which bear witness to the prestige of the leaders of the communities that built them and indicate the high degree of social organization of these communities.

Essentially a passage-tomb consists of a burial chamber which is entered by a passage (52,53), often of considerable length, the whole being covered by a round mound usually surrounded by a kerb (54). Simple chambers of round (e.g. Carnanmore, Co. Antrim), rectangular (e.g. Cross Townland, Co. Antrim), trapezoidal (e.g. Listoghil, Carrowmore, Co. Sligo) or polygonal (e.g. Fenagh Beg, Co. Leitrim) form are well represented but frequently the plan is more complex with cells opening off the chamber (Figure 8). One of the tombs under the great mound at Dowth, Co. Meath has a single side chamber opening from a large circular main chamber but usually the cells are arranged in pairs on either side and an end-chamber opens from the back of the main chamber. The plan with a single pair of side-cells and an end-cell, giving a cruciform design, is a notable component in the Irish passage-tomb repertoire and is found in some of the very finest examples as at Newgrange and Knowth, Co. Meath. This plan though known in Brittany and Iberia can be seen, if not as an Irish speciality, as a standardization in Ireland of tendencies present on the continent. Besides the cruciform plan more complex plans with two or even three pairs of side-cells are fairly well represented. For these close comparisons with French sites are possible.

Sills frequently divide the passage into segments and are also

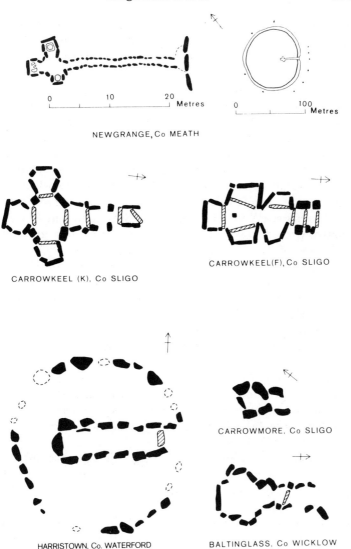

Figure 8 Plans of passage-tombs
Newgrange and Carrowkeel (K): cruciform plan; Carrowkeel (F)
multiple cell; Baltinglass and Carrowmore: simple passage-tombs;
Harristown: undifferentiated passage-tomb.

found across the entry to the side-cells, as in some of the tombs at Loughcrew, Co. Meath and Carrowkeel, Co. Sligo. The very small tomb at the Mound of the Hostages at Tara, Co. Meath, is divided into three segments, each about 1.25 m square, by low sills and each segment is floored by a single tight-fitting flag. Here the distinction between passage and chamber is scarcely discernible save for a slight increase in the height and the somewhat heavier construction of the inmost segment.

The passages, being narrow, were roofed in a simple manner with lintels but the chamber in the more elaborate tombs was usually roofed in a dome fashion by corbelling — a technique already referred to in connection with souterrains and clocháns. While the corbelling was sometimes built of relatively small stones as at the Mound of the Hostages, it was generally of large slabs and the roofs, when intact, are impressive pieces of construction. The excellence of the work and the height — rising to nearly 6 m above the ground — makes the Newgrange roof one of the most impressive features of this great monument (59), rivalled only by the magnificent roof of the cruciform tomb discovered in 1968 under the great mound at Knowth. The corbels of the centre chamber and the lintels of the passage in Newgrange are supported on dry-stone masonry, in front of which are upright stones which give no support to the roof but serve to hold firm the dry-stone walling and the cairn material behind and also serve to provide suitable flat surfaces for the carvings which are a feature of this and so many of these tombs.

The greatest tombs are of gigantic proportions — the mound at Newgrange is about 80 m in diameter and over 12 m high and the passage and chamber extend underneath it for a distance of 24 m, while the two recently discovered tombs under the great mound at Knowth are both considerably longer. However, most passage-tomb mounds are of much more modest dimensions, less than 30 m in diameter, and the overall length of some chambers and passages can be as little as 4 m to 5 m. In construction also the passage-tombs range from the complex corbelling to simpler forms where the capstone rests directly on the orthostats of the chamber walls. These simple forms, which are found in large numbers in Carrowmore,

Co. Sligo (67) but are also represented elsewhere, e.g. Antrim and Down (31), have evidence for short or vestigial passages only and some appear to have no passages. Though some writers tend to regard these types as distinct from the passage-tomb series several factors demand their inclusion within it. Firstly, they occur in cemeteries where not only are similar structures with passages present but also more complex chamber forms — for instance there is a tomb with passage and side chambers in Carrowmore itself. Secondly, finds identical with those typical of the Irish passage-tombs were discovered in some of them. Finally, in many passage-tomb complexes abroad, e.g. in Brittany and Denmark, closely similar tombs with or without vestigial passages are well represented. To some extent the simple structure may be the result of local geology. The big glacial blocks used at Carrowmore were easily available in the locality as can still be seen from the uncleared slope heavily strewn with boulders on the southern side of the cemetery.

An important aspect of the distribution of passage-tombs (Figure 9) is the preference for hilltop siting and the frequent occurrence of cemetery groupings. Sometimes the tombs are closely grouped as in the great cemeteries on the Boyne or at Carrowmore, Co. Sligo. Sometimes they are more widely diffused on hill or mountain summits with one or two tombs on each, as along the western rim of the Dublin-Wicklow mountains. The main axis of the distribution extends from the district around the mouth of the Boyne to Sligo. Across this axis lie the four great cemeteries at Brugh na Bóinne on the Boyne near Slane, Co. Meath, at Sliabh na Caillighe (Loughcrew) near Oldcastle in the same county, at Carrowkeel, Co. Sligo on the Bricklieve mountains overlooking Lough Arrow and at Carrowmore overlooked by Knocknarea mountain west of Sligo town.

Within the curve of the river Boyne a few miles west of Slane lies the Brugh na Bóinne cemetery dominated by the three great mounds of Newgrange, Knowth and Dowth. Smaller satellite sites lie close to the major tombs and several other mounds largely unexplored (57) lie within the area bounded by the bend of the river. About thirty tombs can be recognized

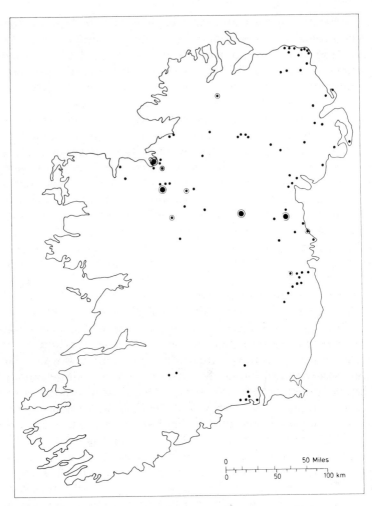

Figure 9   Distribution map of passage-tombs

within this cemetery but this figure is by no means final because, as recent excavations in Knowth have spectacularly shown, many of which no surface trace is apparent may still await discovery and some unopened mounds have yet to be confirmed as passage-tombs. Beyond the cemetery to the north across the Louth border lies the tomb at Townleyhall.

Southwards is the small passage-tomb of the Mound of the Hostages at Tara and near Naul at Fourknocks are a number of round mounds, one of which contains a cruciform passage-tomb with abnormally large ovate central chamber (63). Along the coast southwards of the Boyne there are sites at Gormanstown, Co. Meath, Bremore and a passage-tomb now destroyed at Rush, Co. Dublin.

There were about thirty tombs grouped on and around the summits on the Loughcrew hills which rise sharply some 270 m above the plain. Each summit is crowned by a major site with smaller tombs clustering nearby (54). At Carrowkeel excavations about sixty years ago revealed some fourteen passage-tombs mainly on the crests of the high limestone cliff-lined ridges and there is also a great unopened cairn on Keshcorran the highest peak of the range, together with a few on the lower slopes which should also be included in the cemetery. Carrowmore lies under the shadow of the mountain of Knocknarea, itself crowned by a huge cairn near which are others including one with a cruciform chamber. Here on rolling land scarred by gravel digging are the remains of a cemetery which once consisted of sixty or more sites in a concentration seldom paralleled elsewhere. Though the gravel digging has made the reconstruction of the ancient topography difficult a tendency to place major tombs on commanding sites is to some extent still traceable. Over a wide area in Leitrim, Sligo, Roscommon and extending into south Donegal at Finner, small groups and separate tombs occur, e.g. Fenagh Beg, Co. Leitrim. Many of these crown prominent hills and as at Sheebeg and Sheemore, Co. Leitrim the sites are often clearly intervisible.

Northwards of the Boyne there are small groups of passage-tombs in north Louth (Clermont Mountain) and South Armagh (Slieve Gullion). There are examples in County Down and a series of hilltop cairns in Antrim, e.g. Knocklayd are probably also largely passage-tombs. A group of passage-tombs on the headlands of north Antrim, e.g. Ballintoy (The David Stone) and Cross, are reminiscent in their siting of many Breton passage-tombs. Westwards across Tyrone (Knockmany) to Fermanagh (Belmont Mountain) are a relatively small number of recognized passage-tombs though some other hilltop cairns may conceal chambers. At Kilnamonaster in east Donegal a few recognizable sites remain of what was a cemetery probably of at least a dozen examples.

Southwards of the Boyne on the fringe of the Dublin-Wicklow mountains many summits are or were crowned with passage-tombs. One of these at Seefin (52,53) has several side-chambers and a cairn at Baltinglass which was enlarged by the passage-tomb builders covered three chambers including one of cruciform design and another which suggests a reminiscence of this type (Figure 8). Further south, apart from a site at Derrynahinch, Co. Kilkenny, and the little group of so-called entrance graves near Tramore, Co. Waterford, passage-tombs are rare. Near Aherlow in Co. Tipperary there is a tomb at Shrough and some four miles away at Duntryleague in Co. Limerick a passage-tomb with side cells. A few other prominent mountain-top cairns in this region can also be included. The group of five tombs near Tramore have little or no distinction between the passage and chamber and the burial vault extends almost across the mound, e.g. Harristown (Figure 8) and Carriglong. While such undifferentiated passage-tombs are present in the main Irish series (e.g. at Knowth) the Tramore group compare very closely with tombs in the Scilly Isles and Cornwall and the finds both from these and the Tramore group suggest a late date well within Bronze Age times. It is tempting to see their builders engaged in trade with Scilly and Cornwall for the tin used as an alloy with copper to produce bronze.

The finds recorded from the Irish passage-tombs, excluding the little Tramore group just mentioned, are very consistent. Round-bottomed bowls decorated with looped arcs and other motifs usually executed in a series of deeply impressed stabs have been found in the tombs in all the cemeteries in Meath and Sligo and also at Tara, Baltinglass and elsewhere. Large mushroom-headed pins and neat little pendants, usually of stone, in the form of hammers or stone and chalk balls are of constant recurrence also. Metal or other indications of Bronze Age are absent. Radiocarbon determinations of about 2500 b.c. accord with the material of the finds in ascribing the passage-tombs in Ireland largely to the Neolithic period.

A notable characteristic of Irish passage-tombs is the occurrence on their stones of carved designs. The designs show great variety; circles, arcs, spirals, lozenges, triangles, circles with rays, shield-shaped motifs and others. Two of the great cemeteries have this art to a notable degree — the Boyne (58, 61,62) and Loughcrew. Normally the motifs are executed by pecking but incised lines also occur. At Newgrange and Knowth in several cases the stones have been worked so that the designs stand out in relief. Southwards of the Boyne the art is found at Tara and Fourknocks, Co. Meath (64,65), Seefin, Tournant and Baltinglass, Co. Wicklow and northwards on several sites, Knockmany and Sess Kilgreen, Co. Tyrone and East Torr (Carnanmore), Co. Antrim. It is absent in the great concentrations in the west.

The finest of this decoration, e.g. several stones at Newgrange and Knowth are by any standards true works of art — well conceived, well executed and powerfully composed. In other cases the motifs are rather haphazard and the execution mediocre. We can only guess at the meaning the designs had for the tomb builders. Association with the tombs suggests a sacred and religious symbolism but since we know little or nothing of the decorative tastes of the tomb builders in their houses (perhaps in wood), furniture, or clothing even in this some caution is required. The art clearly belongs to a style which recurs with many variations throughout the whole passage-tomb distribution from Iberia to Scandinavia. In Iberia comparable designs particularly the lozenge, chevron, conjoined arcs and rayed circles are found on schist plaques, cylinder idols and pottery. Engraving on the tombs is very rare but traces of painting are known. The same decorative style is found on pottery in southern France and Brittany. It is only in Brittany and Ireland that the stones of the tombs themselves are profusely engraved. There are many similarities and also notable differences between the Irish and French series but the very presence of the engravings connects the two regions. It can perhaps be said that the Iberian designs, some of which are clearly anthropomorphic, are rather more representational than the French in which, however, we can still recognize human features as well as the representation of axes. In

Ireland, though occasionally the eye or oculus motif can be discerned, the art appears, to us at least, to be very largely abstract. The conjoined arcs on the Irish passage-tomb pottery reflect designs found on the tombs.

Something must be said here of markings found on natural rocks and on large stones forming no part of megalithic tombs. Such rock scribings are usually made by pecking, but some (a small sub-group) are incised. Rock scribings are most frequent in the south-west, especially in west Cork and Kerry (66), but they occur sporadically elsewhere and similar markings are known in Scotland and northern England, in some cases on the coverstones of cist graves. The designs show some similarities to those on the passage-tombs but are in the main of a different type. They consist of cup marks, cup-and-circle patterns, concentric circles with radial lines, rectilinear markings and other motifs. This group of Irish rock scribings has been named 'Galician Art' because of its similarity to the rock art of Galicia in north-western Spain. As Galicia and south-west Ireland are both copper-producing areas it has been suggested that the rock art may have been introduced to Ireland by pre-historic copper miners from north-west Spain.

Satisfactory prototypes for the tomb forms of the Irish series can be found in north-west France, whence the custom of engraving orthostats can also be derived. The Irish passage-tomb builders spread to Anglesey where tombs of identical plan and decoration are found. A few other sites in western Britain are also probably to be ascribed to them but they make no real advances into the great long-barrow districts of southern and eastern Britain.

The passage-tomb builders must to a considerable extent overlap in time with the long-barrow people. Though there is some small evidence of contact we know little of their behaviour one to the other. However, it would appear from their cemetery organization — the sheer size and magnificence of their finest tombs — that the passage-tomb people had advanced more towards civilization than any other Neolithic peoples here. Indeed, in wealth and development they must rank high among their contemporaries in Atlantic Europe.

The last great group of Irish megalithic tombs are the wedge tombs which were formerly called wedge-shaped gallery graves or wedge-graves. They are of rather simpler construction than the court-tombs and passage-tombs and display less variety of design (Figure 10). A division of wedge-tombs into two classes — northern and southern — was for a time widely accepted but it is now clear that though certain features show some variation locally, the whole series forms a very coherent unit. About 400 examples are known (Figure 11). They are very well represented in Munster, west of a line from Thurles to Cork City, where more than half the total are found. A few examples on the Aran Islands off Galway Bay and in West Mayo indicate a weak coastal extension northwards. Inland a more important connection is traceable through east Galway and Roscommon to considerable groups in Sligo and east Mayo. From Sligo and Leitrim they extend in some strength across Ulster from Cavan to Antrim and also northwards into Donegal. They are notably absent in Counties Armagh and Down but about a dozen examples extend from Monaghan into eastern Leinster.

The distribution shows that the wedge-tomb builders preferred light, well-drained soils often in upland regions where forest growth would have been light. The very dense concentration of about 70 tombs on the upper limestone plateau of north-western Clare shows a remarkable coincidence with winter grazing land. These lands which are capable of feeding cattle throughout the year would have been especially valuable to primitive farmers who would not have had hay or root crops for winter fodder. The paucity of wedge-tombs on the shale, flagstone and coal region of west Clare, west Limerick and north Cork and Kerry — probably because of the unsuitability of the land — is in striking contrast not only with the wealth on the limestone but also to the frequent occurrence on the sandstone uplands.

A second factor in the distribution is the notable coincidence in several areas between the tombs and the presence of copper deposits. In the extreme south-west on the peninsulas of Cork and Kerry this is marked. Copper was worked at such places as Allihies, Co. Cork in recent times and ancient workings, some of which may date to Bronze Age times, e.g. Mount Gabriel, are also known. Again in the Silvermines region near

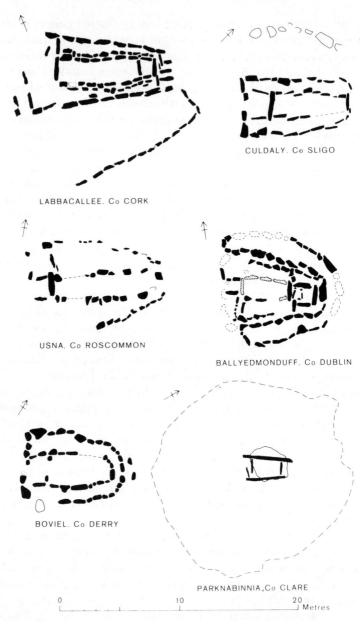

CULDALY. Co SLIGO

LABBACALLEE. Co CORK

USNA. Co ROSCOMMON

BALLYEDMONDUFF. Co DUBLIN

BOVIEL. Co DERRY

PARKNABINNIA, Co CLARE

0   10   20
                                    Metres

Figure 10   Plans of wedge-tombs

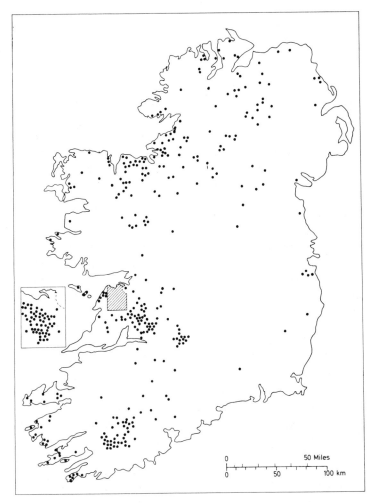

Figure 11　Distribution map of wedge-tombs

Rear Cross in Co. Tipperary the relation of the tomb distribution to the copper is remarkable and there are instances in Mayo (Belderg) and Wicklow where copper is found in the area near wedge-tombs.

The third notable factor in the distribution of wedge tombs is the sharp contrast between it and the distribution of Food

Vessel burials. These burials — discussed in the chapter on burial mounds — belong as do the wedge-tombs to the Early Bronze Age. The two distributions are complementary and to a considerable degree mutually exclusive (compare Figures 11 and 12). The wedge-tombs dominate the west with an upland bias while the Food Vessel dominates in the east and centre especially on gravel and sandy esker regions. This accords with the arrival of the wedge-tomb builders on the west and the intrusion of their Food Vessel contemporaries from the east.

Wedge tombs have long, relatively narrow burial chambers, broader and higher at the entry and tapering to the rear (Figure 10). The entrance faces in a general south-westerly direction. This constant feature is best explained as a general rough alignment of the entrance towards the declining path of the sun from noon to sunset, or alternatively an alignment of the rear of the tomb towards the ascending path of the sun. The orientation of stone circles is closely analogous and the question is referred to again in the chapter dealing with these.

Some wedge-tombs have a single chamber only. In many, however, a portico or ante-chamber at the western end precedes the main chamber and is separated from it by a great septal stone blocking access to the main chamber, e.g. Baurnadomeeny, Co. Tipperary and Glenmakeernan, Co. Sligo. More rarely a closed east end chamber is present, e.g. Labbacallee, Co. Cork (Figure 10), and both portico and east end chamber are found at Ballyedmonduff, Co. Dublin (Figure 10) and the tomb called 'Cashelbane' at Loughash, Co. Tyrone. The great septal slab seems in some cases to be replaced or accompanied by jamb-like stones (Loughash, 'Giant's Grave', but, in some instances at least, these are set as supports for the septal which is often not set in a socket, e.g. Burren, Co. Cavan.

The side walls of the gallery may be formed either of a number of orthostats or of one large slab. The roof slabs normally rest directly on the side stones. Corbelling is present in a few cases only, e.g. Knockshanbrittas, Co. Tipperary, but pad-stones inserted between the roof and sidestones are relatively common.

In north-west Clare, where excellent large slabs are readily available on the surface crag, the majority of the wedge-tombs have one large slab forming each side and a single great roof-stone, e.g. Gleninsheen. This gives a special neatness to the construction especially as the tops of the sidestones are chipped to a straight line (48). They have been described as simple box-like graves; in fact however they possess the wedge-shaped plan, sloping roof and orientation and frequently the outer walling characteristic of the wedge-tomb class as a whole. There is little evidence for porticos in this type and the entrance is usually formed not of one great slab but of two, one crossing about two-thirds of the width, the other outside it closing the gap apparently to function as a door, e.g. Parknabinnia (49 and Figure 10) and Gleninsheen.

Wedge-tombs range in size from diminutive chambers scarcely 2 m long as at Eanty Beg, Co. Clare, to quite lengthy galleries as at Lisduff, Co. Mayo, which is about 9 m in length. They are in general of rather lighter construction than the other Irish megalithic tombs but some are quite impressive. The larger capstone at Labbacallee weighs about 12 tonnes and one of the tombs at Ballyganner, Co. Clare, has sidestones each about 5.50 m long, 1.70 m high and 25 cm thick, while the capstone like that at Clooneen in the same region was of even more massive proportions. At the other end of the scale some diminutive examples are difficult to distinguish from large long cists of a different tradition which will be dealt with in the chapter on burial mounds.

A frequent feature of wedge-tombs is the occurrence outside the chamber sides of an outer-wall set often about 30 cm to 1 m from the sidestones of the gallery. This outer wall which is sometimes higher than the roof of the chamber tends to converge more sharply to the east than do the gallery sides. It frequently runs more or less straight along the sides to join the straight section across the rear of the tomb but in some cases, e.g. Island, Co. Cork (Figure 10) and Loughash, Co. Tyrone, the sides curve inwards to give an elongated U-shaped plan. The outer wall may be doubled as at Labbacallee, Co. Cork and Ballyedmonduff, Co. Dublin (Figure 10). Buttress stones set against the outer wall or directly against the chamber sides have been noted in some sites, e.g. Aughrim, Co. Cavan and

Paddock, Co. Louth. At Baurnadomeeny, Co. Tipperary, excavation showed that the dry-walling between the buttresses was bound by yellow clay almost like mortar.

Where a portico is present the western end of the outer wall is joined to the entrance by a straight facade. In some tombs, notably in Tipperary and Limerick, the outer wall is very close to the chamber sides so that it appears more or less as a doubling of the sides. Excavations at Baurnadomeeny showed that no facade was present and indeed where the outer wall is very close there is no place for an orthostatic link between it and the chamber side. In some cases the frontal facade like the rest of the outer wall may itself be doubled or even trebled as at Ballyedmonduff. There is some evidence to show that in some tombs lacking a portico the outer wall continued across the front thus forming a complete trapeze around the tomb as at Iskancullin and Faunarooska, Co. Clare.

The cairns of wedge-tombs tend to be round or very short oval. Kerbs are rarely in evidence. That defined at Ballyedmonduff, of U-shaped form, suggests a heel-shaped outline for the cairn. However, here as in some other cases an arc of rather heavily bedded stones at the front may indicate that the entrance was originally blocked, giving an ovate, indeed almost circular form to the completed cairn.

Eighteen wedge-tombs in Derry, Tyrone, Leitrim, Dublin, Wicklow, Tipperary, Limerick, Cork and Kerry have been excavated and finds are known from a few others notably from Moytirra in Sligo. Though several, especially in Cork and Kerry, were very poor in finds and produced no primary pottery, the frequent occurrence of Beaker pottery and the barbed- and-tanged arrow-heads which are typical of beaker-using people securely assigns the type to the Early Bronze Age. A coarse bucket-shaped pottery is likewise very frequent. A few metal finds are also present.

The origin of the Irish wedge-tombs can be traced directly to north-western France. Tombs of clearly similar design and orientation are widespread in the Breton peninsula. Though the French sites are often denuded, traces of outer walling so frequent in Ireland are found in a few examples. The finds include Beaker and coarse bucket-shaped pottery, again in agreement with the Irish examples. In Britain, save for one probable example (Bedd Yr Afanc in Wales), the type is unknown.

The more usual burial rite in Irish megalithic tombs was cremation, though unburned burials have also been found in all the major types, usually side by side with cremated remains. In the passage-tombs evidence for a very large number of individuals has been found. At the Mound of the Hostages the two inmost segments had been filled to a depth of about 30 cm with cremated bones among which were several unburnt skulls and other bones. Again at Fourknocks deep deposits of cremated bones filled the cells while the passage contained a large number of unburnt skeletons. In the long-barrow tombs the largest number of burials recorded was at Audleystown, Co. Down where at least 34 unburnt skeletons were repre-sented. In other tombs of the long-barrow and also of the wedge-tomb class smaller numbers, mostly of cremated individuals, were discovered but in some little or no bone was found owing to the acid soil condition.

BURIAL MOUNDS

In dealing with megalithic tombs mention has been made of the mounds of earth or stone which cover or which once covered them. Not all burial mounds, however, contain chambered tombs, and in this section it is proposed to deal with mounds covering other classes of graves and, incidentally, with other burial types.

A burial mound (chambered or unchambered) is usually referred to in this country as a 'tumulus' if built of earth and as a 'cairn' (or 'carn') if it is of stone. Usage is not constant, however, and we sometimes find the word tumulus used to cover both classes of mounds, while the term 'barrow' (used generally in Britain) is applied to the earthen mound. It must be noted, however, that surface appearance gives only limited indications of the material of a mound; a cairn over which a layer of vegetation has grown may look like an earthen mound or the material may be alternate layers of clay and stone heaped up at the original building of the monument or in part piled on to cover later burials inserted near the surface of the primary mound.

Again, it is not always possible to say with certainty if an unexcavated burial mound covers a megalithic chamber or not. In some cases signs of collapse indicate the position of the chamber; the hilltop position of a cairn or its proximity to a group of passage-tombs provide *a priori* reasons for believing it to cover a tomb of this type. A great cairn like that at Knocknarea, near Sligo (about 60 m in diameter) would be presumed to cover a passage-tomb because it is situated in a passage-tomb area and is placed on a summit accompanied by other cairns, in one of which a cruciform passage-tomb is exposed. But all the numerous hilltop cairns which are so conspicuous throughout the country do not contain megalithic tombs. Among the smaller cairns and earthen tumuli, many are certainly unchambered and the graves they cover are varied in type and period.

The burials under burial mounds are sometimes not protected by any structure, their only covering being the material of the mound itself; they are frequently contained in a cist, normally a box-like structure of stone slabs in which an inhumed or a cremated burial is placed. These cists may be either short, i.e. approximately square about 50 cm to 80 cm across (76) or long about 50 cm by 2 m (75). Occasionally cists divided into two compartments occur as at Cavancarragh, Co. Fermanagh and Ballinchalla, Co. Mayo. In general short cists belong to the Early and Middle Bronze Age (Figure 12) while the majority of long cists date from after the end of the Bronze Age into Early Christian times. Long cists were, as their shape suggests, intended to contain inhumed extended burials, but cremations also occur in them. When an inhumed burial is found in a short cist the skeleton is usually in a crouched position — placed on one side with the knees drawn up towards the chin (74). In Ireland many crouched burials are accompanied by Food Vessels (though, of course Food Vessels are not confined to this type of burial); in England they are accompanied by Beakers. At any rate we can see these cists as representing a single-grave tradition opposed to the collective burials of the megalithic tombs.

A relatively small number of single burials, usually under round mounds, have been assigned to the end of Neolithic times. Classic examples such as Drimnagh, Co. Dublin, Ballintruer, Co. Wicklow and Linkardstown, Co. Carlow, had large central cists of irregular polygonal shape with inward sloping sidestones and heavy coverstones. In most cases layers of highly pitched slabs closely surrounded the sides and oversailing stones, reminiscent of corbels in megalithic tombs, sometimes lay between the sidestones and the cover. Exceptionally as at Norrismount, Co. Wexford, the cist was of rectangular plan but the overlapping corbel stones were present. In most examples the mound was of complex structure, with a core of stones or sods around the cist. Over this core a mantle of earth or sods was piled. Kerbs surrounding the mound were noted in some cases. At Jerpoint West, Co. Kilkenny and Baunogenasraid, Co. Carlow, besides the outer kerb, two internal settings of stones concentric with the kerb were placed within the

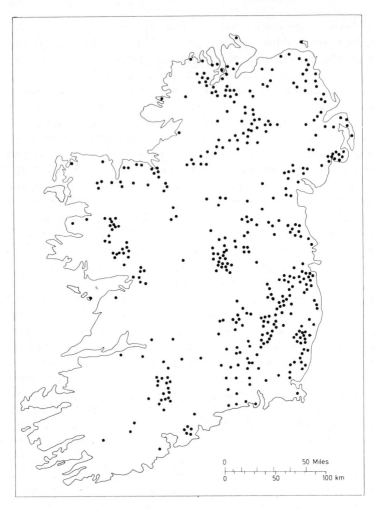

Figure 12   Distribution map of Early Bronze Age
cists (after Waddell)

mound. Excavation at the latter side showed that the outermost kerb was added when the mound was enlarged for
secondary burials. The mounds in most examples were fairly
uniform in size from 22 m to 25 m in diameter though that at
Norrismount was about 35 m as was the mound which

surrounded the large cist, excavated in 1838, at Knockmaree in the Phoenix Park, Dublin. At Rath, Co. Wicklow, a rectangular double cist and another burial, which seems to have been enclosed in an irregular cist, lay in a circular knoll, about 60 m in diameter and 5 m high, which appears to have been largely natural.

Most of these cists contained a skeleton of an adult male. A specialized, highly decorated, round-bottomed vessel with sharply inturned neck accompanied the skeleton. Similar vessels from three sites: Kiltale, Co. Meath; Dunn Ailinne, Co. Kildare and Rathgall, Co. Wicklow, may indicate comparable burials but no evidence for cists was present. At Linkardstown, Drimnagh and Jerpoint West plain Neolithic ware was also found showing an overlap with the classic Neolithic A tradition. No pottery was reported from the central cist at Knockmaree which, exceptionally, contained two skeletons but a bone toggle in the shape of a barbell corresponds to one from Jerpoint West.

These sites lie in a band from Meath to south Kilkenny along the flanks of the Dublin-Wicklow massif, with one, Norrismount, to the south of the mountains in Co. Wexford. A recent discovery of a site at Ardcrony, north-east of Nenagh, Co. Tipperary, extends the distribution westwards. The area occupied is in general lowland and the sites lie between 30 m and 180 m above sea level. However, they are generally placed in relatively commanding positions, usually on ridges or hilltops and the siting compares with that of Irish passage-tombs and many Bronze Age cairns.

The single burial mode represents a sharp break from the megalithic tradition of collective burial and despite differences in detail, in pottery and to some extent in cist form, accords with that current in the Early Bronze Age, especially with the unburned burials such as are frequent with Food Vessels of the Bowl class.

Besides the Leinster group a few other Neolithic sites in the single burial tradition are known in Munster. At Rathjordan, Co. Limerick, in a pit, under a round earthern mound surrounded by a fosse, a plain shouldered Neolithic bowl was found which may have accompanied a burial and in the same neighbourhood, within the famous settlement site on Knockadoon at Lough Gur, a crouched skeleton of a youth was found with a large decorated Neolithic bowl buried in a pit. The first period of a complex site at Moneen, Co. Cork, has been assigned to the Neolithic on the basis of pottery finds but the pottery in question is more easily interpreted as Cinerary Urn belonging to the Middle Bronze Age.

Round mounds frequently contain Bronze Age burials, sometimes in cists, sometimes unprotected. Both cremated and unburned bones occur. In some instances a number of burials are found in the mound. Such monuments are called multiple-cist cairns or preferably cemetery mounds. A cairn at Knockast, Co. Westmeath, contained forty-three burials. Five cists containing cremations were built in various parts of this mound but most of the interments both burned and unburned were unprotected. There did not appear to be any central cist. Frequently, as at Beihy, Co. Fermanagh, a large central cist is present and a number of other burials are placed elsewhere in the mound. Thus at Mount Stewart, Co. Down, a large rectangular cist which was devoid of grave goods when explored, was central in the mound and some fifteen other cists, several of which contained Food Vessels, lay concentrated in one quadrant. At Poulawack, Co. Clare, a large central cist formed of several layers of overlapping slabs and six other cists lay in a hilltop cairn with multiple kerbing. A complex site at Dún Ruadh, Co. Tyrone, consisted of a cemetery cairn surrounded by a fosse and bank. Sherds of Neolithic A ware in pits under the cairn represented pre-cairn activity. In the cairn, which apparently was hollow in the centre, were at least ten cists which yielded fine Food Vessels of the Bowl class.

The custom of placing many burials in one mound is well established in Early and Middle Bronze Age times. Sometimes as at Poulawack, Co. Clare, a sequence can be observed with some burials placed during the construction of the cairn and others inserted later. This, of course, is not the same as the re-use of mounds of an older tradition referred to below. It is rather to be considered as the use of the mound as a cemetery for successive burials by the same community.

In cemetery mounds Food Vessel pottery is predominant. These vessels are placed with the burials, usually in an upright position. It is thought they held offerings of food or perhaps more probably drink for the departed. Sometimes Cinerary Urn burials are also present. These larger vessels are normally placed mouth downwards and over the cremated remains. Though essentially a new rite introduced after the Food Vessel people were well established, a degree of fusion between Food Vessel and Cinerary Urn users is apparent.

The practice of multiple individual burial led to the insertion of such burials as secondaries in pre-existing mounds of various types. The Mound of the Hostages (77) had a large number of such burials accompanied by Food Vessels and Cinerary Urns inserted in it and the innermost compartment of the original passage-tomb was cleared of its burials to accommodate Food Vessels interments. Again, at Fourknocks in the same county, several Bronze Age burials were inserted in the mound of a passage tomb. Re-use of the mounds of other types of megalithic tombs is also occasionally found. For example, at the court-tomb in Doohatty Glebe, Co. Fermanagh, some fifteen secondary cists were reported and at the portal-tomb of Aghnakeagh (A), Co. Louth, six cists lay within a mound which may have been altered to receive them. The mound of a wedge-tomb at Kilmashogue, Co. Dublin, was enlarged for secondary Food Vessel burial and a Cinerary Urn burial was intruded into the portico. Similarly in some examples of Neolithic cist burials later intrusions are found. At Drimnagh, a layer of sand was added in which an urn burial was placed while at Baunogenasraid the mound was enlarged to receive Food Vessel burials.

Frequently a burial or cemetery of the Early to Middle Bronze Age with Food Vessel and Cinerary Urns is found without any surface mound. Such burials may be in cists or simply in pits. They are normally discovered by accident as a result of ploughing, sand digging, land clearance or such activities. Some quite extensive flat cemeteries have been recorded, e.g. Edmondstown, Co. Dublin, with 18 burials; Cloughskelt, Co. Down, 24 burials; Ballyenahan, Co. Cork, 17 burials; Ballinchalla, Co. Mayo, 6 cists; and Keenoge (74),

Co. Meath 14 burials, 6 of which were in cists. Many flat cemeteries occur in eskers and in some cases natural hillocks in the ridges may have, as it were, substituted for mounds. Frequently a cist or an unprotected single burial appears to have been placed alone but it is often uncertain whether or not other undiscovered burials exist in the vicinity. The number of sites where one burial only was recorded is large and this itself suggests that such burials were quite common.

Apart from the type of Bronze Age (Food Vessel and Cinerary Urn) burials, unmarked graves of a wide variety of types and ages come to light. Grave goods where present will provide the best indication of date and context. Both cremation and simple inhumation were practised throughout pre-historic times in Ireland and the mode alone gives little indication of date. However, in the case of unburned remains, a crouched burial, whether in a cist or not would probably be regarded as of Early Bronze Age date but an extended burial without other indication of date must remain very uncertain as to period though many belong to the Iron Age and Early Christian times and of course even later.

The grave goods found with burials in Ireland are scarcely ever of intrinsic value, in contrast to those rich deposits with the dead in say, Egypt, Mesopotamia and other areas. Here they usually consist of pottery vessels, small bronzes (knives or razors), stone implements or ornaments (beads or pendants), or bone ornaments.

Though as we have noted, earth is used to a considerable degree in the structure of some of the mounds already discussed, mounds almost entirely of earth require separate treatment. Such mounds, preferably called earthen barrows rather than tumuli may to some extent reflect the availability of materials but their occasional occurrence in areas where stones are widely used for other mounds, e.g. near Carrowmore, Co. Sligo and Loughcrew, Co. Meath, seems to indicate some difference in custom. It is usual to find around an earthen barrow a fosse from which the material of the mound was taken by the builders (80) but some tumuli are built of material — earth or sods — transported from elsewhere and not taken from a surrounding fosse. The fosse may not be

59   NEWGRANGE: ROOF OF CHAMBER SHOWING CORBEL TECHNIQUE

60   NEWGRANGE: SIDE-CHAMBER SHOWING BASIN STONE

61 NEWGRANGE: DECORATED CORBEL AND PORTION OF ROOFING-
STONE OF SIDE-CHAMBER

62 NEWGRANGE: TRIPLE SPIRAL

63   PASSAGE-TOMB AT FOURKNOCKS, CO. MEATH, SHOWING CENTRAL
CHAMBER AND PASSAGE

64 FOURKNOCKS: DECORATED LINTEL

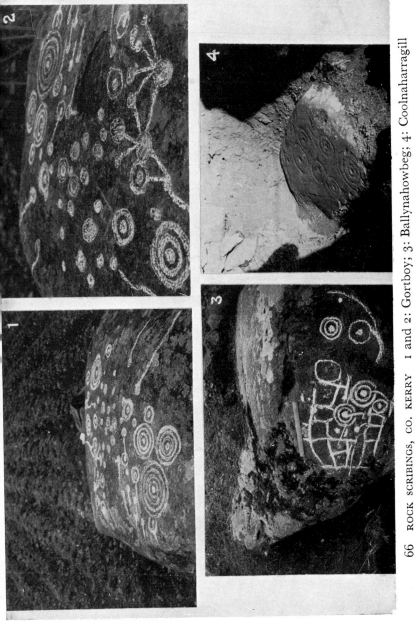

66 ROCK SCRIBINGS, CO. KERRY   1 and 2: Gortboy; 3: Ballynahowbeg; 4: Coolnaharragill

67　PASSAGE-TOMB, CARROWMORE, CO. SLIGO

68　PORTAL-TOMB, LEGANANNY, CO. DOWN

69   PORTAL-TOMB, HAROLDSTOWN, CO. CARLOW

70   PORTAL-TOMB, BALLYNAGEERAGH, CO. WATERFORD

71 STONE CIRCLE WITH ENCLOSED BOULDER BURIAL AT KENMARE, CO. KERRY

72 STONE ALIGNMENT, 'FINN MAC COOL'S FINGERS', SHANTEMON, CO. CAVAN

73   MEGALITHIC CIST FROM CHAPELIZOD, CO. DUBLIN
(now in Zoological Gardens, Dublin)

74   CIST BURIAL, KEENOGE, CO. MEATH, SHOWING SKELETON AND FOOD
VESSEL

75   LONG CIST GRAVE AT CUSH, CO. LIMERICK—BROKEN FOOD VESSEL IN POSITION

76   SHORT CIST GRAVE AT CUSH—URN IN POSITION

77 'MOUND OF THE HOSTAGES', TARA, CO. MEATH

78 BARROW AT RATHJORDAN, CO. LIMERICK

79   TUMULUS AT LATTIN, CO. TIPPERARY

80   TUMULUS AT CUSH, CO. LIMERICK—DURING EXCAVATION, SHOWING
FOSSE

83 STONE WITH IRON AGE ORNAMENT, TUROE, CO. GALWAY

82 OGHAM STONE, MINARD, CO. KERRY

81 STANDING STONE, PUNCHES-TOWN, CO. KILDARE

84 INSCRIBED STANDING STONE, BALLYVOURNEY, CO. CORK

86 STONE CIRCLES, GRANGE, LOUGH GUR, CO. LIMERICK

87   STONE CIRCLE, DROMBEG, CO. CORK

88   LISSYVIGGEEN STONE CIRCLE, KILLARNEY, CO. KERRY

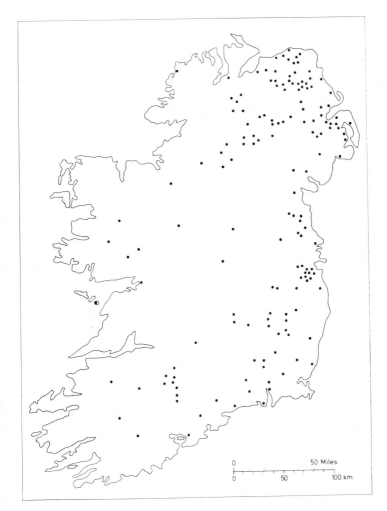

Figure 13   Distribution map of cinerary urns (after Kavanagh)

recognizable before excavation because it has become filled with soil which has silted into it.

In southern Britain, where earthen round-barrows are very numerous, elaborate classifications based on the variety of their forms have been proposed. When the fosse immediately surrounds the base of the mound or when there is no fosse we have the simplest form of tumulus — known in Britain as a 'bowl-barrow', because of its resemblance to an upturned bowl. Where a flat space exists between the fosse and the mound the type is known as a 'bell-barrow'. Several other varieties of barrow, known to British archaeology (particularly in Wessex where they have been well studied), have not been recognized here, but one form which consists of a low mound (4 m to 15 m in diameter) surrounded by a ditch and outer bank may be equated with the 'saucer-barrow' or when the mound is very slight or non-existent is better referred to under the name 'ring-barrow'. (This is the equivalent of the terms used in the Netherlands — *Kringrep* — and in Germany — *Kreisgrab*).

These ring-barrows are well known in the flat areas of County Limerick and some have been noted elsewhere. Frequently they are barely perceptible, having been flattened due to ploughing and other causes. In other cases the mound, ditch and bank may be well marked. Pottery of Neolithic type has come from some of these monuments at Rathjordan, Co. Limerick (78), Early Bronze Age sherds from others at the same place and one at Lissard, Co. Limerick, produced the remains of an urn (Middle Bronze Age) inverted over cremated bones. This burial rested on the old ground surface near the centre of the barrow. Of the many examples of these barrows excavated in Limerick, only this one at Lissard produced any evidence of burial — in others there was presumably an inhumed body so lightly covered that it disappeared without leaving any trace.

A number of barrows excavated in the west of Ireland illustrate well several varieties of barrow form, and also demonstrate that though the finds from some show a remarkable consistency others, of more or less comparable form, belong to widely differing contexts.

Ten round earthen barrows in Carrowjames townland, Co. Mayo, lay on marshy land in the bottom of a valley between two low esker ridges. They were in two closely set groups. The first group consisted of three barrows each surrounded by a fosse. These measured about 15 m in overall diameter and 50 cm high. The fosses were about 2 m wide and 30 cm to

45 cm deep. The material of the mound was earth with a somewhat stony central core. In the centre of each was a pit dug apparently when the mound was partially piled up. These pits contained the primary cremation in two cases with a Cinerary Urn of the Cordoned variety. In all three cases a bronze razor accompanied the primary cremation. The mouth of the central pit was closed by a slab in two instances and in all three barrows spreads of charcoal occurred at higher levels and other cremated bones were scattered in the mounds. The finds securely date the first use of these barrows to the Middle Bronze Age, about 1400 b.c.

The second group of seven barrows lay some 80 m to the south-east. One which was cut in two by a road was not excavated. Four were small, 6 m to 8 m in overall diameter and scarcely 25 cm high and like those of the first group described above no bank appeared outside. The remaining two excavated sites were surrounded by a fosse with a low external bank. One was 21 m in overall diameter and 50 cm in height. No formal central pit was present but three widely scattered cremations were spread in the body of the mound. At the outer edge of the external bank a Cinerary Urn burial was found, perhaps contemporary with, but quite possibly pre-dating the barrow. Finds of flint and chert arrow-heads, hollow-based and leaf-shaped, would not be inconsistent with a Bronze Age date. The other barrow with external bank measured 15 m in overall diameter and was only 25 cm high. Numerous pits dug into the subsoil under the barrow contained cremations associated with finds of Iron Age date. A single chert barbed-and-tanged arrow-head found in the body of the mound is not sufficient to cast doubt on the ascription of this barrow to the Iron Age. Finds from the four smaller barrows, referred to above, were meagre. They contained cremations sometimes in pits, some scattered in the mound. In one case a broken iron object found with scraps of cremated bone, though not of course definitive, tends to confirm the general probability that some at least of the scattered cremations are Iron Age.

In the neighbouring County of Galway, at Carrowbeg North, two mounds which compare with the Middle Bronze Age examples at Carrowjames were excavated. Each was surrounded by a fosse and measured about 17 m in overall diameter. They were about 1 m high, considerably higher than those at Carrowjames, and in one instance this height was greatly augmented by the fact that the mound was built on a natural knoll in the esker. In the first example a core of stones about 7 m in diameter covered a centrally-placed pit dug into the subsoil. This contained the primary cremation accompanied by a bronze razor. Similarly under the centre of the second mound was a shallow pit containing a few fragments of cremated bone and close by in a second pit a neat short cist 55 cm by 40 cm and 30 cm high was built. This contained a cremation with a flint knife of a type often associated with Early and Middle Bronze Age burials. In the fill of the deep rock-cut fosse lay four extended skeletons.

In Co. Galway also, at Pollacorragune near Tuam, an earthen round-barrow covered in a thin layer of stones and measuring 8 m in diameter and 1.25 m high, was sited on the top of an esker. Under the centre was a cremated burial contained in a fine cordoned Cinerary Urn which was placed mouth downwards over the bones. A finely decorated bronze razor lay with the cremation. In another barrow nearby, four extended skeletons were buried in shallow trenches dug into the underlying gravel. These lay on their backs with the heads to the north-west. Fragments of iron found with the skeletons prove that they were post-Bronze Age in date.

Burials belonging to the Late Bronze Age in Ireland are virtually unknown save for one example recently discovered within the great hill-fort at Rathgall, Co. Wicklow. Here, three cremations placed in pits were found within a circular area, 16 m in diameter, enclosed within a fosse. In one case the cremated bones were contained in a coarse flat-bottomed pottery vessel. A slab acted as a cover for the vessel and another larger slab lay over this.

Iron Age burials, though less well attested than those of the Neolithic or Early and Middle Bronze Age, are becoming increasingly known. Besides the instances in the west of Ireland already mentioned, examples are reported from Grannagh and Oranbeg in Co. Galway. At Grannagh, in a round mound enclosed by a ditch and external bank, cremations were found scattered on the mound. Recent excavations have confirmed an Iron Age date for this site and for that at Oranbeg. Other burials dated to Early Iron Age times have been found in larger barrows of the ring-barrow type excavated at Carbury Hill, Co. Kildare. The ritual enclosures on the Curragh, Co. Kildare, are essentially enlarged specimens of ring-barrows — one produced an extended burial but the burial was probably dedicatory. There is no clear dividing line between large ring-barrow and earth-circle ritual site. At Lugg, Co. Dublin, a site enclosed by bank and (outer) fosse was used successively as ritual and burial place. The burial under one of the Cush, Co. Limerick, tumuli was merely a scatter of cremated bones on the old ground surface where the cremation pyre had been lit, and over which the mound had been built. Under a second tumulus at the same site (80) the cremated bones had been collected into a hole in the old ground surface and with them had been placed a small bone plaque (also showing signs of burning) bearing Early Iron Age ornament.

It is clear from the above account that round burial mounds can contain interments of a wide variety of types and ages, ranging over the whole prehistoric period, and that a single site may include a number of distinct phases with burials of more than one tradition represented. There has been in the archaeological literature a tendency to refer to unchambered round mounds as a Bronze Age type, in contradistinction to the chambered mounds thus implicitly ascribed to the Neolithic — an over-simplification for both classes.

In particular low barrows of the ring-barrow type yield little information as to date and context from surface indications. Even excavation has failed in many cases to yield such information. The paucity of finds may in part be due to their vulnerability to disturbance by tillage and to soil conditions inimical to the preservation of bones. In some cases even with comparatively rich finds like the Neolithic Early Bronze Age pottery from two sites in Ballingoola, Co. Limerick, it is not possible in the absence of evidence for burial to state categorically that the sites were sepulchral. The need for caution in assuming a funerary function for such monuments was brought out by the fact that another site in the same townland

proved on excavation to be a hut of uncertain date. Several of
the rings surveyed at Lissard which lay within a ring-fort might
be similarly interpreted. They appear to be later than the ring-
fort but the question of their nature and function must be left
open.

Even more surprising were small sites, superficially like ring-
barrows on the Curragh of Kildare, which unlike other earthworks excavated there, proved not to be prehistoric at all but
army cooking places of the nineteenth century. In the Pollacorragune district of Galway, not far from the genuine burial
cairns described above, a number of 'barrows' were examined.
Most yielded little result while a few proved to be cooking
places perhaps of eighteenth century or later date.

One class of cairn continued to be built until recent times,
and the custom still prevails in places, but the cairns are not
for burials. They are memorials in commemoration of an
event such as a violent death, and are due to the practice of
each passer-by throwing a few stones on a pile at the site of the
happening commemorated. The same custom is followed at
certain cairns which form 'stations' on a *turas* where 'rounds'
are made in honour of a saint, as at Glencolumbkille, Co.
Donegal.

STANDING STONES

The simplest type of monument with which we deal is the standing stone, which, as its name implies, is merely a stone set upright in the ground. The standing stone is variously known to archaeology as a 'monolith' or 'menhir' and in Irish as 'Gallán', 'dallán', or 'liagán'. Examples in Ireland range in height from less than a metre to about six metres. Not only is the standing stone a simple form of monument, but also the idea underlying its erection is such a simple one that its simplicity warns us against ascribing it to any one period of cultural context.

The erection of a modern gravestone is essentially similar to the erection of an ancient standing stone, and indeed serves the same purpose as did some of those. Excavation has revealed that standing stones in some cases mark ancient burials. The tall standing stone at Punchestown, Co. Kildare (81), which fell some forty-five years ago and was re-erected, was found to have at its foot a small cist grave. Again, at the centre of the Longstone Rath (an enclosure mentioned again under 'Stone Circles') a standing stone stood beside a long cist grave. Both graves are Bronze Age in type and the finds from the Longstone Rath indicate a date in the Early Bronze Age. More recently, cremated bone was discovered at the base of a standing stone at Drumnahare, Co. Down, and at Carrownacaw in the same county, excavation showed that a ring-ditch some 6 m in diameter closely adjoined a fine pillar about 3 m in height. In the filling of the ditch were traces of cremated bone, a fragment of pottery and some flints while further flints including transverse arrow-heads were found in the vicinity of the base of the stone. An Early Bronze Age date seemed probable. Excavation at a third stone in Co. Down at Ballycroghan revealed a cist measuring about 2 m by 1 m set 2.50 m from the base of the stone. The excavation around a standing stone near Newgrange, Co. Meath, produced a number of flints a few of which were worked.

But not all examples were erected to mark burials. It has been concluded that some served as boundary marks, while others may mark the line of ancient roadways as in the case of a series of standing stones near Lough Gur, Co. Limerick. It is also thought that some were raised to mark the sites of notable events.

It is clear that certain standing stones were invested with a sacred character as is shown by their presence on ancient ceremonial sites such as the inauguration place at Magh Adhair, Co. Clare, and at Tara. Certain highly ornamented stones of Early Iron Age date (with La Tène ornament carved on them) at Turoe, Co. Galway (83); Castlestrange, Co. Roscommon and Killycluggin, Co. Cavan, were undoubtedly cult objects. Superstitious practices are said to have been associated with some holed standing stones. These are simple uprights perforated with a hole, sometimes natural and sometimes artificial, a few centimetres in diameter.

Other standing stones carry inscriptions in ogham characters (see below) or Early Christian crosses or dedications (84, 85). One cannot, of course, conclude that these inscriptions are always as old as the time of the erection of the stone; some of them may have been inscribed at a later date, but in other cases the stones were certainly erected specifically to bear the inscriptions. The standing stone at Kilnasaggart, Co. Armagh, has on it crosses, crosses in circles and an inscription. The inscription gives evidence to date the memorial to about the beginning of the eighth century — a late date for the erection of so crude a memorial.

This span of dating evidence — from Bronze Age burials to Early Christian inscriptions — shows that standing stones in Ireland cannot be ascribed to any one period. Presumably the impetus to their erection in the first instance came from the megalithic cultures which brought the custom of building the great stone tombs, but the date of any single example can only be decided from the evidence it yields to examination (from inscriptions or associations of the site) or excavation. It is likely that even excavation would, in many cases, leave unsolved the question of date. However, recent survey gives an indication that at least in certain areas, e.g. Cork and Kerry, where standing stones are especially numerous (over six hundred are known), many may well belong to the same tradition as that of the stone circles and alignments.

Uninscribed standing stones are very numerous in Ireland and are widely distributed. It is noteworthy, however, that they occur most densely in areas such as Co. Cork and Central Ulster where the main concentrations of stone circles, described in a later chapter, are found. Ogham stones on the other hand are most densely concentrated in the south from Kerry to Waterford and south Leinster where about seven-eighths of the 350 or so known examples occur. There are also a few Irish ogham stones in western Scotland while to the east in Pictland a series of enigmatic inscriptions in ogham characters, probably nineth century a.d. in date, have defied interpretation. On the Isle of Man and in southern Britain, principally in Wales and Cornwall ogham inscriptions are well represented. In these areas the Irish name written in ogham is frequently accompanied by a Latin inscription written in Roman characters whereas in Ireland the inscriptions are in ogham only.

The language of the ogham inscriptions is Irish in an early form. The inscriptions are commemorative, i.e. the name of the person commemorated is given followed frequently by the name of father and ancestor. The letters are represented by lines and notches, from one to five in number, marked on either side of or across a stem line. There are five main groups of letters as shown in Figure 14. On a standing stone one or more corners is used as a stem line. In the majority of cases the inscription reads from bottom upwards.

Reading is perfectly easy if one is dealing with a clear-cut inscription. But since the inscription has, in almost all cases, become imperfect through wear or spalling of the stone, its interpretation is best left to an expert who has had long practice. The observant worker may, however, be fortunate enough to discover a hitherto unknown inscribed stone. Such have been found built into farm buildings or used as gate posts, and as already noted, they are frequently found forming the roofing stones of souterrains.

The context of ogham stones is largely Christian. Many are

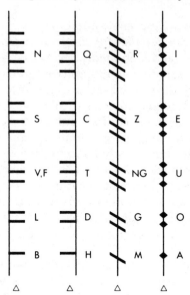

Figure 14 Ogham alphabet

found in Christian church or burial sites and many are inscribed with crosses. They date principally from the early fifth century to the middle of the seventh century. The custom of erecting ogham stones as memorials or grave stones may have originated among the Irish colonists in Wales and spread to Ireland with Christianity. The distribution in Ireland suggests a connection with the areas where Christianity was established by missionaries other than St Patrick, e.g. St Ciaran of Saighir and St Declan of Ardmore.

STONE ALIGNMENTS

Alignments consist of groups of standing stones arranged in one or more straight lines. They are of rather restricted distribution in Ireland and elaborate forms are rare here, but they are well represented in south-west England, Wales and Scotland and above all in Brittany where very imposing examples occur. Finds from the few examples excavated in Ireland at Beaghmore, Co. Tyrone and Drumskinny, Co. Fermanagh, are rare as is indeed the case with examples excavated abroad, e.g. Cholwichton in Devonshire, and we can only conclude, probably correctly, that stone alignments are monuments connected with prehistoric ritual.

Alignments occur in two main regions in Ireland — Tyrone, Derry and Fermanagh in the north and Cork and Kerry in the south. In the northern group they occur usually placed more-or-less tangentially to stone circles. They extend upwards of 150 m in length. They are composed of comparatively low stones often one metre or less in height. Elaborate complexes including alignments, circles, cairns and cists as at Beaghmore, Co. Tyrone, may be compared with examples on Dartmoor in Devon such as Marivale. An isolated alignment, known as 'Finn MacCool's Fingers', impressively sited on a hill three miles north-east of Cavan town (72), lies considerably outside the main northern group.

The Cork and Kerry alignments form part of the great complex of monuments, stone circles, boulder burials etc. discussed in the next chapter. They consist of from three to six standing stones placed roughly in line. Short examples are only a few metres in overall length while the longest recorded in this group is about thirteen metres long. The heights of the stones within each alignment are unequal. Frequently a grading in height from one end to the other is apparent but this is by no means a constant feature. The individual stones range from a metre or even less to about four metres high. A good example of an alignment is found at Castlenalact, near Bandon, Co.

Cork, while another occurs at Beenalaght north of Donaghmore in the same county. Occasionally alignments adjoin stone circles. For instance, at Cabragh, north of Macroom, Co. Cork, an alignment of four massive stones stands close to a small stone circle and a similar combination is found at Cashelkelty, Co. Kerry.

Recent survey has increased the number of alignments known in the Cork-Kerry region to over fifty-five. They are aligned roughly north-east and south-west and when their orientations are plotted show a pattern very similar to that found in the stone circles (see next chapter) and wedge-tombs. The pairs (see below) conform to the same orientation pattern.

The pairs of standing stones which occur frequently in the Cork-Kerry region may be abbreviated alignments. Excellent examples are found at Coolcoulaghta near Durrus and Keilnascarta near Bantry. As with the alignments, pairs are found beside stone circles, e.g. Kealkil, Co. Cork. Pairs are also known in several different parts of the country and may have had in some cases a special cult significance, but in others they can be shown to be nothing more than the gate posts of an ancient enclosure which has been cleared away. An example occurs near Kilfinnane, Co. Limerick, where two standing stones ·mark the entrance to a destroyed ring-fort, the outline of which may be discerned when the site is looked at from a neighbouring hillside. Similarly, a pair of stones defines the entrance to a cillín at Oughtihery, near Rylane, Co. Cork.

In relation to standing stones and stone alignments, a word of warning is necessary. Sometimes a single standing stone or an alignment may not have been erected originally as such. It may in fact be the only remaining part of quite a different structure, most of which has been destroyed, such as a megalithic tomb, a stone circle or an ancient field fence built with upright stones. A further difficulty arises in the matter of standing stones, since it was the custom to erect stones such as these in recent times as scratching posts for cattle. Tradition is frequently a guide in this matter, but in some districts it may be of little help, especially where the words *Gallán* or *liagán* are no longer in use. In these instances, the individual example must be considered on its merits, and one is helped by the general appearance of the stone and perhaps by its relation to other antiquities.

A concentration of almost three hundred standing stones extending over many acres in the townlands of Timoney Hills and Cullaun, near Roscrea, Co. Tipperary, serves as an example where special difficulty of interpretation has arisen. Except for one possible circle of some sixteen uprights they form no sensible plan at present. Certain features cast doubt on the site as being an ancient monument. Many of the stones are loosely set and a stone somewhat like a partially made millstone lies near an arrangement of diminutive set stones within the 'circle'. Local tradition records that there was widespread land clearance about the middle of the last century in the very fields where the stones occur and thus confirms the view that the stones were erected in modern times.

STONE CIRCLES

While we have not in Ireland any stone circle as imposing as the English examples at Stonehenge and Avebury we have considerable numbers of stone circles which tend to concentrate in certain parts of the country (Figure 15) and which are related in origin and in function to those grander and more famous examples of Great Britain. While many of the Irish circles are small, we have also, as we shall see, some big and imposing sites.

The term 'stone circle' suggests at once the class of monument in question. These monuments consist essentially of a circle of stones enclosing an open area, or, possibly, a space in which there is a small burial mound or a stone-built grave. It is well to anticipate here the discussion on function and to state that the term 'stone circle' implies a monument primarily dedicated to ritual. Stone circles must be differentiated from monuments presenting to the casual observer a similar appearance but serving a different purpose. A stone fort with partially demolished ramparts may sometimes look like a stone circle, as may also a circular stone hut site. Even more difficult is the problem presented by the stone kerb of a burial cairn when the cairn itself has been removed (55). In fact, the sites of cairns of which only the kerbs remain were sometimes marked 'circles' on the Ordnance Survey Maps, for instance at Carrowmore, Co. Sligo.

Stone circles in Ireland are of varied forms. Typical of the west Cork area, where they are very common, are circles of free-standing uprights which vary in number from five to seventeen while the diameter of the circle ranges from 2.50 m to about 17 m. The entrance to these stone circles is in the north-east between a pair of matched stones which are the tallest in the monument. Diametrically opposite the entrance is a stone called the 'axial stone' or 'recumbent stone', which is the lowest stone in the monument. This stone is usually set on its side rather than on end and has a straight horizontal upper

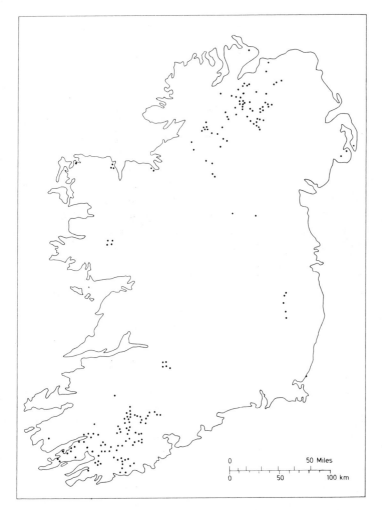

Figure 15 Distribution map of stone circles (after Ó Nualláin)

edge. The name 'recumbent stone circle' was originally applied to Scottish examples, discussed below, where very large recumbent stones are a marked feature. It is a surprising fact that outside the Cork-Kerry region and a possible example at Beltarry, Co. Donegal, referred to below, the recumbent stone is known only in eastern Scotland, in Aberdeenshire, where it is found in stone circles of rather different type. The Scottish circles are of larger diameter and enclose burial cairns. The recumbent stone is in the south-west arc of the circle as it is in the Irish examples. However, in Scotland it is flanked by the two tallest stones of the circle, whereas in Ireland the tallest stones are on the opposite side. In Ireland there is a regular grading of height westwards from the entrance stones down to the recumbent, while the grading in the Scottish examples is in the opposite direction.

There are over ninety stone circles recorded in Counties Cork and Kerry. About half of these are small, about 2.50 m to 4 m in diameter and consist of five stones only. These monuments, though clearly members of the stone circle group, are usually more D-shaped than circular, often emphasized due to the length of the recumbent in proportion to the diameter. The rest of the Cork-Kerry stone circles with seven or more stones average about 10 m in diameter and are usually quite accurately laid out. In a few cases the entrance, besides being marked by tall uprights, is formed of stones set outside the perimeter as at Gowlane North, near Donoghmore, Co. Cork, where four stones form an entry passage. Three of the large type of stone circle, all in the vicinity of Glandore, Co. Cork, have been excavated, Drombeg (87) (seventeen stones), Bohonagh (thirteen stones) and Reanascreena (thirteen stones). A five-stone example was excavated at Kealkil near Bantry. Here a small cairn covering a circle of small set stones, placed concentrically within the circumference, was found immediately beside the stone circle while a pair of large standing stones stood close by. The same feature occurs at Lissyviggeen (88), near Killarney, where a circle of small diameter with seven uprights is surrounded by a bank, outside which stand two outliers.

The occurrence of complexes of associated monuments consisting of circles, outliers, alignments, cairns and boulder burials is a feature of the Cork-Kerry region. A notable grouping at Knockraheen, north of Macroom, contains a five-stone circle with two outliers, a cairn with radially set stones surrounded by a fosse together with two other small cairns.

Recent survey has demonstrated the widespread association

of boulder burials with the stone circle series of Cork and Kerry. A boulder burial consists of a cover stone, usually about 2 m long by 1 m wide and 1 m thick, placed on very low supporting stones which often scarcely protrude above ground level. Excavation of an example near the stone circle at Bohonagh, Co. Cork, showed that a cremated burial was placed under the cover. The capstones of boulder burials can resemble capstones of megalithic tombs especially of the Carrowmore passage-tomb type but the supports do not make clearly defined formal chambers. There are now over fifty boulder burials recognized in Counties Cork and Kerry. In eight instances they occur within stone circles, usually singly, but as many as four are grouped together in the Breenymore circle not far from the site at Kealkil mentioned above. In a few other cases boulder burials are set near circles as at Mill Little, north of Bantry, Co. Cork, but often they appear to be isolated as on Clear Island.

The stone circle complex including boulder burials has a somewhat different distribution in Cork and Kerry to that of the numerous wedge-tombs in the same region. However, like the tombs a relationship of the distribution of the stone circle complex with areas rich in copper is apparent.

Another centre of concentration of stone circles is County Tyrone and the neighbouring areas of Fermanagh and Derry. These circles are usually composed of smaller stones than those in the County Cork ones, but the number of stones is greater. The normal diameter is somewhat less than 15 m. The largest of the stones are usually only 1 m or so in height while the majority may be quite low — about 30 cm — or may even be small boulders. Many of these stone circles have stone alignments associated with them; these are usually placed tangentially (or approximately so) to the circle. These stone circles are found on upland areas, above the 150 m contour, and they are frequently covered (completely or partially) by a growth of peat, their existence, in some cases, being unsuspected until revealed by turf cutting.

The most remarkable stone-circle site in County Tyrone is that at Beaghmore, north-west of Cookstown. The remains here were only very incompletely appreciated before the turf was removed in the course of excavation. It is now known that they extend over several acres and the area uncovered has revealed a complex system of circles, small cairns, and alignments. Excavations at Drumskinny, Co. Fermanagh, revealed a complex consisting of a stone circle with tangential alignment and a cairn. At Castledamph, Co. Tyrone, a complex stone circle with an alignment set not tangentially but in line with the diameter was excavated. Within the circle was a small low cairn covering a cist containing cremated bones.

Stone circles of various types occur in the neighbourhood of Lough Gur, Co. Limerick, and these include some of the most remarkable in the country. The most striking and the best known of the Lough Gur examples is the great circle (in Grange townland) on the western side of the lake (86). This is defined by a contiguous (i.e. placed edge to edge) ring of standing stones about 45 m in diameter. Outside these is a bank which gives the uprights support and which is 9 m in width and rises to a height of 1.20 m against the stones. Some of the stones forming the circle are immense, the largest being a great upright, rectangular (over 1 m by 2 m) in cross-section, and 4.20 m in total height, more than 1.50 m being sunk in the ground. Nor was the erection of the stones and the piling up of the great bank the total work of the ancient builders; they also covered the whole interior of the circle with clay to a depth of as much as 60 cm so as to hide the unsightly packing stones placed at the base of the uprights and to provide a level space within. The entrance through the bank was lined at either side with small uprights and gave access to the interior between two large portal stones. The excavation of this site gave important results to which reference will be made below in connection with the discussion on date.

Another circle on the eastern side of the lake (in Lough Gur townland) is almost as large as the one described; it has a great bank with upright stones at either side of it and at the centre a ring of stones concentric with the outer ones. Excavation showed that a fosse (now silted up) existed inside the bank and that the material for the bank had been taken from the fosse.

Of a different type are those of the Lough Gur circles composed of a ring of separately placed boulders instead of upright stones. One of these (in Grange townland) has a low mound within it, a similar neighbouring site has no mound nor has the large example at Ballynamona some miles south-east of Lough Gur.

The localities mentioned, though they include the main centres of concentration of stone circles, do not by any means cover the total distribution of stone circles in Ireland. A number occur in the Kildare-Wicklow border area, and these include some very fine examples characterized by stones of considerable size. At Athgreany, near Hollywood, Co. Wicklow, is a partially ruined stone circle with a large block lying some 40 m downhill from it which may have been an outlier. At Broadleas, Co. Kildare, is a large circle, 30 m in diameter, on a low hill summit, while a somewhat smaller circle once stood in the nearby townland of Whiteleas. At Castleruddery, Co. Wicklow, is an excellent example some 25 m in diameter within a well-preserved bank in a manner reminiscent of the great stone circle at Grange, Co. Limerick, while at Boleycarrigeen, Co. Wicklow, is a neat stone circle about 4 m in diameter surrounded by a low bank.

Stone circles are known in County Louth. In County Down there is a fine example at Ballynoe, referred to again below, which encloses a burial cairn, and at Castlemahon in the same county the remains of a stone circle about 11 m in diameter enclosed a central pit near which was a cist containing the cremated remains of a child. The splendid circle on a hilltop at Beltany, near Lifford, Co. Donegal, encloses a cairn and has a huge stone on its western side, suggesting comparison with the Scottish recumbent stone circles. Close to the well-known stone with Iron Age design at Killycluggin, Co. Cavan, is a stone circle, but there is no indication as to its relationship to the carved stone. In the same neighbourhood in Kilnavert townland are small circles of boulders on the summits of hillocks.

A few stone circles are known along the north Mayo coast. There is a small group at Rathfran on Killala Bay, one of which was destroyed about twenty-five years ago, and an isolated example, some 5 m in diameter, at Glengad about twenty-five miles to the west. In the Cong district of County

Mayo, close to the Galway border, are a number of stone circles. One has two concentric rings, a second has a fosse and bank, a third stands on top of a low mound while the fourth is a circle composed of a number of three-stone arrangements each with two tall stones flanking a lower one. A remarkable site at Masonbrook, Co. Galway, consists of a bank with seven standing stones set radially on it. The nature of this site is somewhat doubtful because there is on record that the stones were re-erected and excavation did not yield evidence of date.

The custom of surrounding a burial mound with a circle of stones is shown in its most impressive form at Newgrange where twelve great standing stones remain out of a probable total of thirty-four, placed somewhat excentrically with the kerb of the cairn (56). At Ballynoe, Co. Down, a fine stone circle surrounds a mound which appears to have been of long-barrow type. This phenomenon of a ring of stones encircling a burial mound is of interest in relation to the origin and affinities of the stone circle, but before dealing with this matter consideration must be given to the date of stone circles in Ireland.

Stone circles are notoriously disappointing in the matter of dateable finds. No evidence of date was obtained in several excavated sites — the large stone circle east of Lough Gur, the Kealkil site and the similar one at Knocknakilla on Muisire Beag Mountain, Co. Cork. Of the three larger stone circles excavated in County Cork only one, Drombeg, produced a dateable artefact — a coarse pottery vessel of a type found in Neolithic and early Bronze Age contexts. The circle and alignment at Castledamph, Co. Tyrone, produced no dateable artefacts. The extensive site at Beaghmore yielded a stone axe and a few fragments of pottery of Neolithic character. At the comparable complex at Drumskinny a hollow-scraper and a potsherd possibly Neolithic in type were found. The largely destroyed circle at Castlemahon yielded good Neolithic ware from a pit on the perimeter and a flint knife of Early Bronze Age type from a burial near the centre. At Ballynoe a sherd of passage-tomb (Carrowkeel) ware was found but it is not clear whether it belonged to the circle or the cairn enclosed within it.

Fortunately, however, abundant material came from one site — the great stone circle in Grange townland, west of Lough Gur. A considerable amount of pottery was found, mainly in the neighbourhood of the uprights where it had, perhaps, been broken ritually, as seems to have occurred on some of the Brittany monuments. On the Lough Gur site there were also flints, stone axes, bone points and some bronze. The pottery included Beaker, among which was a vessel (an A-Beaker) which closely resembled one discovered in Somerset, as well as other (B) types similar to those found on the Lough Gur habitation sites. With the Beaker were other classes of pottery, some of Neolithic type and notably examples of well-developed Food Vessel. The material gives a date in the Early Bronze Age, say about the twentieth century b.c. and the different types of pottery suggest that different groups of people co-operated in the construction of the monument. Excavation showed that this circle had not been used for habitation and had no burials — negative evidence which indicates its having been built for ritual purposes.

The clear dating — to Beaker times — of one example does not imply that all Irish stone circles are of this date. However, the finds from the other sites though few are quite consistent with such a dating to a time when the Neolithic way of life was giving way to that of the Bronze Age Beaker users. It agrees also with the main body of evidence for the stone-circle cult in Britain.

In the present state of knowledge, exact prototypes for the Irish and British stone circles cannot be cited from the continent. Indeed, apart from a group on the sea shore at Er-Lannic in Brittany the type is scarcely known on the mainland of Western Europe. However, it is possible to point to certain clear traditions which must have contributed to the stone circle complex in both Britain and Ireland.

The megalithic contribution to the origin of stone circles can be readily acknowledged in view of what we have learned of the structure of megalithic tombs. The use of uncut stones — often of great size — and the consummate skill with which they were handled are surely a heritage from the megalithic tomb builders. Just as it can be argued that the great standing stones (menhirs) and alignments for which Brittany is famous owe much to the traditions and example of the tomb builders there, so also the same megalithic tradition influenced the development of the insular circles, alignments and standing stones. In particular, the boulder burials associated with the Cork-Kerry group, are probably, as has been indicated above, descended from simple passage-tomb forms.

The other element that must be sought in any attempt at the derivation of stone circles is the idea of a circular enclosed space. In Britain ritual enclosures including some classes of stone circles are grouped under the word 'henge'. This term is derived from Stonehenge and from its wooden counterpart, discovered by aerial photography, for which the name 'Woodhenge' was coined. Strictly speaking the word henge is applicable to monuments with lintels on the uprights — a feature for which Stonehenge alone presents evidence — but the term is, by extension, used to cover all sites with free-standing circular settings of posts or stones surrounded by ditch and bank or even with ditch and bank only.

There are in Ireland a number of embanked enclosures to which the name henge has sometimes been applied. An example at Monknewtown near Slane, Co. Meath, consisted of a broad earthen bank about 11 m wide enclosing a circular area some 80 m in internal diameter. There was no fosse inside or outside. Within the enclosure were several burials in pits sometimes with stone cists protecting them. In one sector there was evidence for habitation and an oval hut with floor sunken below ground level. The finds from this site were predominantly within the Beaker tradition with traces of some plain Neolithic ware. A notable exception was a pot of distinctive Carrowkeel (passage-tomb) ware which contained a cremated burial. Several comparable enclosures are known in the same region. A much denuded example lies on the banks of the Boyne near Newgrange and another near the passage-tomb of Fourknocks. Near the great tomb at Dowth is a huge bank enclosing an area about 140 m in diameter. Another fine example has been reported from Stackallen about 10 km to the west.

The correspondence between the distribution of these sites

with the great passage-tomb concentrations in the Boyne region and the position of most of them in the vicinity of the tombs is striking. One outstanding example of the type is known outside the Boyne region — the 'Giant's Ring' at Ballynahatty, Co. Down. Here an enormous earthen bank forms a circular enclosure about 180 m in diameter. Near the centre of the enclosure is a passage-tomb.

The characteristic features of the type (very large diameter, the apparent lack of fosses — though Micknanstown, Co. Meath, may perhaps have an internal fosse — and a siting in positions not suggestive of defence) help to distinguish the type from univallate hill-forts and large ring-forts. Inevitably, however, doubt must exist in certain cases. Rath Maeve at Tara, Co. Meath is a case in point. It is on the whole probable that the enclosing bank lacks a fosse, though interference by field drains make for uncertainty. There are indications that some of the material of the bank was scarped from the interior. In these circumstances it is more likely that this site should be classed with the embanked enclosures rather than with hill-forts but only excavation can decide the issue. Another site, Longstone Rath, Co. Kildare, has often been included with the embanked enclosures. Here a large ring-fort of normal design encloses a hilltop on which a cist and standing stone are situated. The finds from the cist indicate an Early Bronze Age (Beaker) context but it is most unlikely that a fully developed ring fort would occur at such an early date. The monument, therefore, most probably represents two distinct periods separated by many centuries. A third enigmatic site is the Sillagh Ring south of Naas, Co. Kildare. It lies on a hillslope and is incomplete either because of partial destruction or more probably because its builders left it unfinished. A decision as to its nature and function is well nigh impossible without excavation.

The finds from Monknewtown immediately suggest comparison with the occurrence of Beaker and related wares on the skirts of the great passage-tombs of Newgrange and Knowth. It has been suggested that the great stone circle encompassing the Newgrange cairn belongs to the Beaker-using people. It could therefore, like the embanked enclosures, represent the incoming of Beaker users attracted perhaps by the wealth and achievements of one of the richest passage-tomb regions in Europe. The great stone circle at Grange, Co. Limerick, with a bank without a fosse has obvious affinities with the enclosures discussed and indeed might be accepted as a member of the general class. The fact that it uses a circle of stones — many of gigantic proportions — links again the stone circle and the embanked enclosures. The less impressive example at Castleruddery, Co. Wicklow, does likewise.

The embanked enclosures with internal fosse on the Curragh, Co. Kildare, appear to have been ritual and to date from the Iron Age. It is probable that they relate more to the barrow burials than to the great enclosures discussed above.

The idea of a ritual enclosure is, of course, not inconsistent with the burials that are found in some stone circles and enclosures. However, even if we suppose a ritual purpose we are far from being able to say in what the ritual consisted. Circles were presumably places of assembly for the population groups to whom they belonged and such assemblies were, doubtless, occasions of ceremonial and conclave. For parallels to these ceremonies we might invoke the practices of modern primitive peoples whose dances take place around structures similar to our circles but the comparison, valid probably on broad lines, is not likely to help in the matter of detail.

The use of stone circles as observatories or as centres of sun worship has frequently been discussed and we must allow for some magical or religious purpose connected perhaps with seasons or feasts. Further evidence of the use of some circles in this manner has sometimes been adduced from their orientation, e.g. the alignment of the main axis towards the rising or setting sun on a particular day of the year. There is no doubt that some degree of orientation was considered important by prehistoric man not only in stone circles but in some megalithic tombs; its importance has been obscured by the extravagant claims made by its protagonists who have sometimes argued about orientation as if Neolithic and Early Bronze Age man used modern precision instruments. General rather than precise alignments — as in the case of churches and Christian burials — would explain the orientation of stone circles as also of megalithic tombs.

BIBLIOGRAPHY

Abbreviations used

CLAJ	*County Louth Archaeological Society, Journal*
JCHAS	*Cork Historical and Archaeological Society, Journal*
JGAHS	*Galway Archaeological and Historical Society, Journal*
JKAS	*County Kildare Archaeological Society, Journal*
JKerryAHS	*Kerry Archaeological and Historical Society, Journal*
JRSAI	*Journal of the Royal Society of Antiquaries of Ireland*
NMAJ	*North Munster Antiquarian Journal*
OKR	*Old Kilkenny Review*
PPS	*Proceedings of the Prehistoric Society*
PRIA	*Proceedings of the Royal Irish Academy*
RM	*Ríocht na Mídhe*
TRIA	*Royal Irish Academy Transactions*
UJA	*Ulster Journal of Archaeology*

Much of the literature relating to Irish field antiquities is contained in Irish archaeological journals, a list of which will be found in *JRSAI* 105 (1975). Useful syntheses of work up to the end of the Second World War, with copious references to the literature are R. A. S. Macalister, *The Archaeology of Ireland*, London, 1928; A. Mahr, 'New Aspects and Problems in Irish Prehistory', *PPS* 3 (1937), 261-436 and S. P. Ó Ríordáin, 'Prehistory in Ireland 1937-1946', *PPS* 12 (1946), 142-71. Ó Ríordáin's third and fourth editions of *Antiquities of the Irish Countryside* contain extensive references to the principal works up to 1953. For the most part references before 1953 are not included in the lists that follow. The works mentioned are selected not only for the accounts they contain but also for the bibliographical information they provide.

General works

M. Herity and G. Eogan, *Ireland in Prehistory*, London, 1977, is a most useful synthesis from the earliest times to the Iron Age. It is fully illustrated and contains a comprehensive bibliographical index. Brief accounts of Irish archaeology will be found in *Encyclopedia of Ireland*, Dublin, 1968. An essay on 'The Prehistoric World' in *A View of Ireland*, Dublin, 1957, 149-64, published after the author's death, gives an interesting summary of Professor Ó Ríordáin's views on Irish prehistory. L. N. W. Flanagan, *Ulster*, London, 1970, is a well illustrated summary of the prehistory of the northern half of Ireland with a gazetteer of important sites. G. F. Mitchell, *The Irish Landscape*, London, 1976, provides a valuable account of the Irish scene throughout the ages and provides a most useful context for the understanding of settlement. E. R. Norman and J. K. S. St Joseph, *The Early Development of Irish Society*, Cambridge, 1969, is useful in illustrating the use of aerial photography. For the historic period see F. Henry, *Irish Art in the Early Christian Period (to 800 A.D.)*, London, 1965; *Irish Art during the Viking Invasions (800-1020 A.D.)*, London, 1967; *Irish Art in the Romanesque Period (1020-1170 A.D.)*, London, 1970. M. and L. De Paor, *Early Christian Ireland*, London 1967. Ll. Laing, *The Archaeology of Late Celtic Britain and Ireland c. 400-1200 A.D.*, London, 1975.

Excavations

Most of the excavation reports which form a large part of the literature on Irish field antiquities are published in *PRIA*, *JRSAI*, *UJA* and *JCHAS*. E. E. Evans, *Prehistoric and Early Christian Ireland — A Guide*, London, 1966, includes very convenient short summaries of results of most Irish excavations prior to 1965. Preliminary annual reports on Irish excavations from 1955 to 1966 appeared in *PPS* 22-7 (1956-61). From 1961 the preliminary reports were published in the Annual Reports of the Royal Irish Academy. Since 1969 the publication *Excavations* (ed. T. Delaney) provides a most useful annual summary of work in Ireland.

Guides

E. E. Evans, *Prehistoric and Early Christian Ireland — A Guide*, London, 1966. Killanin and Duignan, *Shell Guide to Ireland*, London, 1969, contains notes on monuments of all periods throughout Ireland. Harbison, *National Monuments in the Republic of Ireland*, Dublin and London, 1970, covers monuments in state care in the Twenty-Six Counties and a selection of others not in state care; useful notes on means of access to the sites are given. These works have each introductory accounts of the various monument types and the archaeological and historical context. For monuments in the Six Counties of Northern Ireland see *Ancient Monuments of Northern Ireland in State Care*, H.M.S.O., Belfast, 1962 and *Ancient Monuments of Northern Ireland not in State Charge*, H.M.S.O., Belfast, 1952.

Surveys

Only one systematic comprehensive archaeological survey of a county has yet been published: E. M. Jope (ed.), *An Archaeological Survey of County Down*, H.M.S.O., Belfast, 1966. Such surveys are completed or nearing completion in Counties Armagh, Fermanagh, Louth, Meath and Westmeath. The publication of these and the completion of the survey of all Ireland are most pressing needs. Chart (ed.), *A Preliminary Survey of the Ancient Monuments of Northern Ireland*, H.M.S.O., Belfast, 1940, remains a valuable guide to the principal monuments of the Six Counties. M. J. O'Kelly, 'Survey of the Antiquities in the Barony of Small County, Co. Limerick', *NMAJ* 3 & 4 (1942-4); Liam Price, 'The Ages of Stone and Bronze in the County Wicklow', *PRIA* 42C (1934), 31-64 and D. Mc' O'Brien, 'A List of Archaeological Sites on the Berehaven Peninsula', *JCAHS* 75 (1970), 12-14, are useful contributions. Of the work of earlier generations T. J. Westropp's many articles in *JRSAI* and *PRIA* from 1887 to 1920 give accounts, often with plans and illustrations, of hundreds of monuments of many types in Clare, which contribute greatly to a full archaeological survey of that county.

Field archaeology

The following works, though concerned mainly with Britain, provide useful introductions to the study of Irish monuments. *Field Archaeology in Great Britain*, Ordnance Survey, Southampton, 1973. Eric S. Wood, *Collins Field Guide to Archaeology in Britain*, London, 1968. J. X. W. P. Corcoran, *The Young Field Archaeologist's Guide*, London, 1966.

Forts

T. J. Westropp, 'The Ancient Forts of Ireland', *TRIA* 31 (1896-1901), 579-730. This is the most comprehensive account of Irish forts, and gives adequately the state of knowledge regarding them at the beginning of the century. Numerous other papers by the same author mainly in *PRIA* and *JRSAI* deal with forts of special areas and with headland forts of the whole coast.

Ring-forts:

V. B. Proudfoot, 'The Economy of the Irish Rath', *Medieval Archaeology* 5 (1961), 94-121 and 'Irish Raths and Cashels: Some Notes on Chronology, Origins and Survivals', *UJA* 33 (1970), 37-48, contain comprehensive bibliographies of excavated sites. For some recent discussions see G. F. Barrett and B. J. Graham, 'Some Considerations Concerning the Dating and Distribution of Ring-forts in Ireland', *UJA* 38 (1975), 33-47 and M. J. O'Kelly, 'Problems of Irish Ring-forts' in *The Irish Sea Province in Archaeology and History*, Cambrian Archaeological Society, 1970.

Hill-forts:

D. M. Harding (ed.), *Hillforts: Later Prehistoric Earthworks in Britain and Ireland*, London, 1976, especially chapter 16 by B. Raftery, 'Rathgall and Irish Hillfort Problems', and by B. Wailes, 'Dún Ailinne: An Interim Report'. See also 'Navan Fort' and 'Dún Ailinne' in *Current Archaeology* 22 (September, 1970). For Tara see S. P. Ó Ríordáin, *Tara: The Monuments on the Hill*, Dundalk, 1968.

Promontory forts:

M. J. O'Kelly, 'Three Promontory Forts in Co. Cork', *PRIA* 55C (1952), 25-59, contains references to T. J. Westropp's numerous papers 1895-1921. V. B. Proudfoot and B. C. S. Wilson, 'Further Excavations at Larrybane Promontory Fort, Co. Antrim', *UJA* 24 & 25 (1961-2), 91-115, with map.

Manx sites:

G. Bersu, *Three Iron Age Round Houses in the Isle of Man* (excavation report), The Manx Museum and National Trust, 1977.

Cillíní:

F. Henry, 'Early Monasteries, Beehive Huts and Dry-stone Houses in the Neighbourhood of Caherciveen and Waterville (Co. Kerry)', *PRIA* 58C (1957), 45-166. M. J. O'Kelly, 'Church Island near Valencia (Co. Kerry)', *PRIA* 59C (1958), 57-136; Fanning, 'Excavations at Reask', *JKerryAHS* 8 (1975), 5-10.

Mottes:
R. E. Glasscock, 'Mottes in Ireland', *Études de castellologie médiévale VII* (Caen 1975), 96-110. R. E. Glasscock and T. McNeill, 'Mottes in Ireland: A Draft List', *Bulletin of the Group for the Study of Irish Historic Settlement* 3 (December 1972), 27-51. T. E. McNeill, 'Ulster Mottes: A Checklist', *UJA* 38 (1975), 49-56.

Moated houses:
T. B. Barry, *The Medieval Moated Sites of South-eastern Ireland: Counties Carlow, Kilkenny, Tipperary and Wexford.* Oxford British Archaeological Reports, 1977.

Fields, roads and linear earthworks

Fields:
V. B. Proudfoot, 'Ancient Irish Field Systems', *Adv. of Science* 14 (1958), 369-71. M. Herity, 'Prehistoric Fields in Ireland', *Irish University Review* (1971), 258-65. S. Caulfield, 'Neolithic Fields — the Irish Evidence' in H. C. Bowen and P. J. Fowler, (eds), *British Archaeological Reports 1978*. M. J. O'Kelly, 'An Island Settlement at Beginnish, Co. Kerry', *PRIA* 57C (1956), 159-94. P. J. Fowler, 'Ridge-and-Furrow Cultivation at Cush, Co. Limerick', *NMAJ* 10 (1966-7), 69-71.

Roads:
P. Tohall, H. C. de Vries and W. Van Zeist, 'A Trackway in Corlona Bog, Co. Leitrim', *JRSAI* 85 (1955), 77-83. E. Rynne, 'The Danes' Road, a Togher near Monasterevin', *JKAS* 13 (1961-3), 449-57; 'Toghers in Littleton Bog, Co. Tipperary', *NMAJ* 9 (1965), 138-44; 'A Togher and a Bog Road in Lullymore Bog', *JKAS* 14 (1964-5), 34-40.

Linear earthworks:
E. E. Evans, *Prehistoric and Early Christian Ireland — A Guide*, London, 1966, see under 'Travelling Earthworks'. O. Davies, 'The Black Pigs Dyke', *UJA* 18 (1955), 29-36. E. M. Jope, (ed.), *An Archaeological Survey of Co. Down*, H.M.S.O., Belfast, 1966.

Souterrains

No comprehensive work on Irish souterrains has yet appeared. Since souterrains occur frequently in ring forts, many accounts of ring forts include descriptions of souterrains. A large number of examples are described in numerous short articles in *UJA*, *CLAJ*, *NMAJ*, *JGAHS*, *JKerry AHS* and *RM*. The following articles contain preliminary county lists. Co. Louth: Ó Ríordáin B., 'The Souterrains in County Louth', *CLAJ* 13 (1953-6), 441-50. (A number of further examples are described by E. Rynne, in several subsequent articles in the same journal and one by D. C. Twohig, in *JCHAS* 76 (1971), 131-3.) Co. Westmeath: E. Rynne and E. Prendergast, 'Two Souterrains in Co. Meath' (with list), *RM* 2 (1962), 37-43. E. Rynne, 'Souterrain at Fore, Co. Westmeath (list of Westmeath souterrains)', *RM* 3 (1964), 118-23. Co. Waterford: E. Rynne, 'Souterrain at Lisarow, near Ardmore, Co. Waterford' (with list of reference to published examples in the county), *JCHAS* 67 (1962), 28-32. Co. Kerry: J. Waddell, 'Notes on some Kerry Souterrains' (with list). For County Down and Antrim see *UJA* especially A. E. P. Collins and D. M. Waterman. For Co. Down also *An Archaeological Survey of County Down*, H.M.S.O., Belfast, 1966. Several Cork souterrains are listed by D. C. Twowig, M. Walsh and E. M. Fahy in *JCHAS* 1953-76.

House sites

S. P. Ó Rírdáin, 'Lough Gur Excavations: Neolithic and Bronze Age Houses on Knockadoon', *PRIA* 56C (1954), 297-459. A. ApSimon, 'An Early Neolithic House in Co. Tyrone', *JRSAI* 99 (1969), 165-8. S. Ó Nualláin, 'A Neolithic House at Ballyglass near Ballycastle, Co. Mayo', *JRSAI* 102 (1972), 49-57. F. Henry, 'Early Monasteries, Beehive Huts and Drystone Houses in the Neighbourhood of Caherciveen and Waterville, Co. Kerry', *PRIA* 58C (1957), 54-166. L. De Paor, 'A Survey of Sceilg Mhichíl', *JRSAI* 85 (1955), 174-87. C. Ó Cuileanáin, 'Excavations of a circular Stone House at Glannafeen, Co. Cork', *JRSAI* 85 (1955), 94-9. P. McCaffrey, 'Some Stone Hut-circles in the Barony of Dunkellin', *JRSAI* 86 (1956), 187-91. Several ring fort excavations have yielded evidence for houses and huts.

Coastal dwelling sites

G. F. Mitchell, 'Further excavation of the Early Kitchen-Midden at Sutton, Co. Dublin' *JRSAI* 102 (1972, 151-9. A. E. P. Collins, 'Further Investigations in the Dundrum Sandhills', *UJA* 22 (1959),

5-20. B. Ó Ríordáin and E. Rynne, 'A Settlement Site in the Sandhills at Dooey, Co. Donegal', *JRSAI* 91 (1961), 58-64, see also *JRSAI* 92 (1962), 158-9. G. D. Liversage, 'Excavations at Dalkey Island, Co. Dublin, 1956-59', *PRIA* 66C (1968), 53-233. M. J. O'Kelly, 'A Shell Midden at Carrigtohill, Co. Cork', *JCHAS* 60 (1955), 28-32.

Ancient cooking places

The classic account is M. J. O'Kelly, 'Excavations and Experiments in Ancient Irish Cooking Places', *JRSAI* 84 (1954), 105-55. See also E. Fahy, 'A Hut and Cooking Place at Drombeg, Co. Cork', *JCHAS* 65 (1960), 1-17. H. W. M. Hodges, 'The Excavation of a Group of Cooking-places at Ballycroghan, Co. Down', *UJA* 18 (1956), 17-28. E. Prendergast, 'Prehistoric Cooking Places in Webbsborrough District, Co. Kilkenny', *OKR* (1955), 1-10 (with list for Kilkenny). M. Ryan, 'Fulachta Fiadha near Kilnaboy, Co. Clare', *NMAJ* 10 (1966-7), 218-9.

Crannógs

W. G. Wood-Martin, *The Lake Dwellings of Ireland*, London, 1886, remains essential. Besides the excavations before 1953 (listed in the earlier editions of the present work) see A. E. P. Collins, 'Excavations at Lough Faughan Crannóg, Co. Down', *UJA* 18 (1955), 45-80. For preliminary report on the important site at Rathtinaun, at Lough Gara, Co. Sligo, see J. Raftery, 'Iron Age and Irish Sea: Problems for Research' in C. Thomas (ed.), *The Iron Age in the Irish Sea Province*, C.B.A. Research Report 9, London, 1972. Collins and Seaby, 'Structures and Small Finds discovered at Lough Eskragh, Co. Tyrone', *UJA* 23 (1960), 25-37.

Megalithic tombs

Three volumes of the full Megalithic Survey of Ireland have been published: R. de Valera and S. Ó Nualláin, *Survey of the Megalithic Tombs of Ireland*, Vol. I (Co. Clare), Vol. II (Co. Mayo), Vol. III (Cos Galway, Roscommon, Leitrim, Longford, Westmeath, Laois, Offaly, Kildare, Cavan), Stationery Office, Dublin, 1961, 1964, 1972. M. Herity, *Irish Passage Graves*, Dublin, 1974 gives a comprehensive account of Irish passage tombs with full inventory of sites and finds. R. de Valera, 'The Court Cairns of Ireland', *PRIA* 60C (1960), 9-140; 'The "Carlingford Culture", the Long Barrow and the

(1960), 9-140; 'The "Carlingford Culture", the Long Barrow and the Neolithic of Great Britain and Ireland', *PPS* 27 (1961), 234-52; 'Transeptal Court Cairns', *JRSAI* 95 (1965), 5-37. For alternative views on court tombs see J. X. W. P. Corcoran, 'The Carlingford Culture', *PPS* 26 (1960), 98-148. Accounts of passage tombs in the Boyne region will be found in S. P. Ó Ríordáin and G. E. Daniel, *Newgrange and the Bend of the Boyne*, London, 1964 and C. O'Kelly, *Illustrated Guide to Newgrange*, Wexford, 1967. For excavations at Newgrange see M. J. O'Kelly, 'Current Excavations at Newgrange, Ireland' in *Megalithic Graves and Ritual* (ed. G. Daniel and P. Kjaerum), Moesgard, 1973. C. O'Kelly, 'Passage-grave art in the Boyne Valley, Ireland', *PPS* 39 (1973), 354-82. For excavations at Knowth see G. Eogan, 'Excavations at Knowth, Co. Meath', *PRIA* 66C (1968), 11-112 and his 'Report on the Excavations of some Passage Graves, Unprotected Inhumation Burials and a Settlement Site at Knowth, Co. Meath', *PRIA* 74C (1974), 299-382.

Burial mounds

For general account of round-barrows P. Ashbee, *The Bronze Age Round Barrow in Britain*, London, 1960. P. McCaffrey, 'The Dunkellin Barrow Group', *JRSAI* 85 (1955), 218-25. J. Waddell, 'Irish Bronze Age Cists', *JRSAI* 100 (1970), 91-139. B. Raftery, 'Freestone Hill, Co. Kilkenny: An Iron Age Hillfort and Bronze Age Cairn', *PRIA* 68C (1969), 1-108. R. Kavanagh, 'The Encrusted Urn in Ireland', *PRIA* 73C (1973), 507-617; 'Collared and Cordoned Cinerary Urns in Ireland', *PRIA* 76C (1976), 293-403. For recent discussion of Late Neolithic Single Burials see Herity and Eogan, *Ireland in Prehistory*, B. Raftery, 'A Prehistoric Burial Mound at Baunogenasraid, Co. Carlow', *PRIA* 74C (1974), 277-312 and M. F. Ryan, 'The excavation of a Neolithic Mound at Jerpoint West, Co. Kilkenny', *PRIA* 73C (1973), 107-27.

Standing stones

See S. Ó Nualláin under Stone Circles below. For Co. Down see *An Archaeological Survey of County Down*, H.M.S.O., Belfast, 1966. For recent excavations at Ballycroghan, Co. Down (p. 21). A. E. P. Collins, 'Excavations at Two Standing Stones in Co. Down', *UJA* 20 (1957), 37-41; 'A Standing Stone at Portaro, Co. Down', *UJA* 39 (1976), 70. E. Shee and D. M. Evans, 'A Standing Stone in the Townland of Newgrange', *JCHAS* 70 (1965), 124-30.

Ogham:

R. A. S. Macalister, *Corpus Inscriptionem Insularum Celticarum*, Vol. I, Dublin, 1945. M. J. O'Kelly and S. Kavanagh, 'A New Ogham Stone from County Kerry', *JCHAS* 59 (1954), 50-3; 'An Ogham-Inscribed Cross-Slab from Co. Kerry', *JCHAS* 59 (1954), 101-10. K. H. Jackson, 'Notes on the Ogham Inscriptions of Southern Britain' in C. Fox and B. Dickins (eds) *Early Cultures of North-West Europe* (Chadwick Memorial Studies), Cambridge, 1950, 199-213.

Stone alignments

See S. Ó Nualláin under Stone Circles below. D. M. Waterman, 'The Stone Circle and Alignment at Dromskinny, Co. Fermanagh', *UJA* 27 (1964), 23-30. A. McL. May, 'Neolithic Habitation Site, Stone Circles and Alignments at Beaghmore, Co. Tyrone', *JRSAI* 83 (1953), 174-97. J. R. Pilcher, 'Archaeology, Palaeoecology and Fourteenth-Century Dating of the Beaghmore Stone Circle Site', *UJA* 32 (1969), 73-91.

Stone circles

S. Ó Nualláin, 'The Stone Circle Complex of Cork and Kerry', *JRSAI* 105 (1975), 83-131, contains a comprehensive treatment of the Cork-Kerry group with full references to excavations and general discussion of Irish Stone Circles. S. Ó Nualláin, 'Boulder Burials', *PRIA* XXXC (1978), 75-114. H. A. W. Burl, *The Stone Circles of the British Isles*, London, 1977. See also A. McL. May and J. R. Pilcher, under Alignments above.

INDEX TO PLACES

The index includes places in Ireland only. Spelling normally follows that used by the Ordnance Survey but in some cases a variant spelling which has been given general currency in archaeological literature is retained. References to photographic illustrations are in italics; grid reference to the map is given by letter and number (e.g. N15).

SUBJECT INDEX